Liberated Parents /
Liberated Children

Liberated Parents / Liberated Children

ADELE FABER

ELAINE MAZLISH

Grosset & Dunlap
Publishers, New York

*To any parent, anywhere,
who's ever muttered to himself,
"There has to be a better way!"*

Contents

PARENTS ARE PEOPLE

Preface

We have had a unique privilege. For over five years we were part of a parent workshop under the personal direction of Dr. Haim Ginott—psychologist, lecturer, and author. He was that rare teacher who was able to present difficult concepts with great clarity, repeated willingly what we needed to hear again, and refreshed us constantly with the excitement of new ideas. In return, he demanded of us that we experiment, share our findings, and explore our own potential.

The results of this experience were far-reaching. As we struggled to shape theory into practice, and practice into personal interpretation, we became aware of changes in ourselves, in our families, and in the members of our group.

To Dr. Ginott, who gave us the skills to be more helpful to our children and more generous to ourselves, we owe much. We can never repay him. What we can do is record our experience and share it with other parents, in the hope that they will take from it what is useful to them.

Acknowledgments

To our children: Kathy, Liz, and John Mazlish; Carl, Joanna, and Abram Faber, for sharing their ideas and feelings with us over the years. Each one, in his own way, has made contributions that have enriched this book.

To Leslie Faber, who spent many hours going over our early drafts, and whose comments and questions invariably led us to rethink, refine, and clarify.

To Robert Mazlish, who read our first awkward writing and saw a finished book. His belief in us helped us to believe in ourselves.

To the members of our group, with whom we exchanged the large and small dramas of our lives. At every meeting we took sustenance from their support.

To our editor, Robert Markel, for his sensitive guidance through each stage of the publishing process.

To Drs. Virginia Axline, Dorothy Baruch, Selma Fraiberg, and Carl Rogers, whose writings have helped us affirm and extend our own experience.

To Dr. Alice Ginott for her warm encouragement and her many helpful comments.

And most particularly, *to Dr. Haim Ginott* for his careful reading of our manuscript, his invaluable suggestions, and for being a continual source of inspiration. We thank him for permission to publish this book based upon his principles of communication with children.

Authors' Note

Almost as soon as we conceived the idea of writing this book, we realized we had a problem: How could we tell our story honestly, and not violate the privacy of either the members of our group or our own families? We decided to create a cast of characters whose experiences would be a composite of our own and other parents we have known. Jan, our narrator, would be the best of us, the worst of us, and although she is none of us, she speaks truly for all of us.

ADELE FABER
ELAINE MAZLISH

Liberated
Parents /
Liberated
Children

Chapter I

In the Beginning
Were the Words

It didn't add up.

If what I was doing was right, then why was so much going wrong?

There wasn't a doubt in my mind that if I praised my children—let them know how much I valued each effort, each achievement—that they would automatically become self-confident.

Then why was Jill so unsure of herself?

I was convinced that if I reasoned with the children—explained calmly and logically why certain things had to be done—that they would, in turn, respond reasonably.

Then why did every explanation trigger an argument from David?

I really believed that if I didn't hover over the children—if I let them do for themselves whatever they could do—that they would learn to be independent.

Then why did Andy cling and whine?

It was all a little unnerving. But what worried me most was

the way *I* had been acting lately. The irony of it all! I, who was going to be the mother of the century—I, who had always felt so superior to those shrill, arm-yanking, "mean" mothers in the supermarket—I, who was determined that the mistakes of my parents would never be visited upon my children—I, who felt I had so much to give—my warmth, vast patience, my joy in just being alive—had walked into the children's room this morning, looked at the floor smeared with fingerpaints, and unleashed a shriek that made the supermarket mother sound like the good fairy. But most bitter to me were the things I had said: "Disgusting . . . slobs . . . can't I trust you for a minute?" These were the very words I had heard and hated in my own childhood.

What had happened to my vast patience? Where was all that joy I was going to bring? How could I have drifted so far from my original dream?

I was in this mood when I came across a notice from the nursery school reminding parents that there was to be a lecture tonight by a child psychologist. I was tired, but I knew I would go. Could I convince Helen to come with me?

It was doubtful. Helen had often expressed her distrust of the experts. She prefers to rely upon what she calls "common sense and natural instincts." Unlike me, she doesn't make as many demands upon herself as a mother, nor does she worry about her children in terms of long-range goals. Maybe it's because she's a sculptor and has outside interests. Anyway, sometimes I envied her easygoing manner, her total faith in herself. She always seems to have everything under control.
. . . Although lately she *has* been complaining about the children. Evidently for the past few weeks they've been at each others' throats, and nothing she says or does makes any difference. It seems that neither her instinct nor common sense

are enough to help her cope with their daily running battles.

As I dialed Helen's number I thought that maybe, with the recent turn of events, she might put aside her prejudice toward the professionals and come with me.

But Helen was adamant.

She said she wouldn't go to another lecture on child psychology if Sigmund Freud, himself, were speaking.

She said she was tired of hearing those pious platitudes about how children must have love, security, firm limits, love, consistency, love, flexibility, love. . . .

She said that the last time she had gone to such a meeting, she walked around the house for three days afterwards nervously measuring her output of "love."

She said she hadn't recuperated sufficiently from that experience to expose herself to any more anxiety-producing generalizations.

A scream came from Helen's end of the phone.

"I'm gonna tell! I'm gonna tell!"

"You tell and I'll do it again!"

"Mommy, Billy threw a block at me!"

"She stepped on my finger!"

"I did not. You're a big dooty!"

"Oh God," Helen moaned, "they're at it again! Anything to get out of this house!"

I picked her up at eight.

The speaker on the program that evening was Dr. Haim Ginott, child psychologist and author of a new book, *Between Parent and Child*. He began his lecture by asking this question: "What is it about the language I use with children that is different?"

We looked at each other blankly.

"The language I use," he continued, "does not evaluate. I avoid expressions which judge a child's character or ability. I steer clear of words like 'stupid, clumsy, bad,' and even words like 'beautiful, good, wonderful,' because they are not helpful; they get in a child's way. Instead I use words that describe. I describe what I see; I describe what I feel.

"Recently a little girl in my playroom brought me a painting and asked, 'Is it good?' I looked at it and answered, 'I see a purple house, a red sun, a striped sky, and lots of flowers. It makes me feel as though I were in the country.' She smiled and said, 'I'm going to make another!'

"Suppose I had answered, 'Beautiful, you're a great artist!' I can guarantee that that would have been the last painting she did that day. After all, where can one go from 'beautiful' and 'great'? I'm convinced: words that evaluate, hinder a child. Words that describe, set him free.

"I also like descriptive words," he continued, "because they invite a child to work out his own solutions to problems. Here's an example: If a child were to spill a glass of milk, I would say to him, 'I see the milk spilled,' and then I'd hand him a sponge. In this way, I avoid blame and put the emphasis where it belongs—on what needs to be done.

"If I were to say instead, 'Stupid. You always spill everything. You'll never learn, will you!' we can be sure that the child's total energy would be mobilized for defense instead of solution. You would hear, 'Bobby pushed my hand!' or 'It wasn't me; it was the dog.'"

At this point, Mrs. Noble, a vocal authority on most subjects in the community, raised her hand. "Dr. Ginott, what you've been telling us is very interesting. But I've always felt that it's not so important what you say to a child as long as he knows you love him. If he feels you really love him, I believe you can say almost anything. I mean, in the final analysis, isn't it love that really counts?"

Dr. Ginott listened thoughtfully. "In your opinion the words themselves aren't so important as long as love is there. I have another view. Suppose you were at a party and accidentally spilled a drink. I suspect it would make a difference if your husband said, even affectionately, 'Clumsy, I see you've done it again. When they hand out awards for house-wrecking, you'll win first prize.' "

Mrs. Noble smiled uncomfortably.

"My guess would be that you would prefer it if your husband said, 'Honey, I see the drink spilled. Can I help you? Here's my handkerchief.' " It was the first time we had ever seen Mrs. Noble at a loss for words.

Dr. Ginott continued, "I do not discount the power of love. Love is wealth. But even with material wealth, we often find that large sums need to be broken down into small currency. In a phone booth a dime is more serviceable than a fifty-dollar bill. For our love to serve our children, we must learn how to break it down into the words that can help them —moment by moment—as when milk spills, or a drawing is offered for approval. And even when we're angry, we can still use the kind of words that do not damage or destroy the people we care about."

Then Dr. Ginott talked about what he termed "anger without insult." He made it clear that it was unrealistic and unnecessary for parents to be patient all the time. He pointed out how it could be helpful for a parent to express his anger—as long as he did not insult the child. In fact, he said, "Our genuine anger is one of the strongest means we have for changing behavior.

"And how do we put this into practice?" he asked. "Once again we use the words that describe. We do not attack personality. For example, if a child's messy room bothers a parent, the parent should feel free to express his genuine feelings—but not with insults and accusations. Not with, 'Why are you such a slob?' Not with, 'You never take care of your things; you've ruined every nice thing I've ever bought for you.' Now it's possible that even with words like these, the child might clean up his room. But he'd be left with resentment toward his parents and a dirty feeling about himself.

"The question is, how could a parent express these same angry feelings helpfully? Again, he could describe. He could say, 'The sight of this room does not give me pleasure!' or 'I see something that makes me angry. Clothes and books and toys belong on the shelf!' or 'When I see things lying all over the floor, I get furious! It makes me feel like opening the window and throwing everything out!' "

A man in the audience raised his hand. "Dr. Ginott," he said, "It seems to me that some of the methods you've been telling about would be more appropriate for a trained professional person. I can't imagine an ordinary parent being able to use this approach."

Dr. Ginott answered him. "I have great faith in 'ordinary' parents. Who has a child's welfare more at heart than his ordinary parent? It's been my experience that when parents are given the skills to be more helpful, not only are they able to use these skills, but they infuse them with a warmth and a style that is uniquely their own."

Dr. Ginott's lecture continued for another half hour. He introduced the idea of being your child's "lawyer." He explained how children had enough judges, jurors and prosecutors; and he gave examples of the ways parents could be "attorney for the defense." He elaborated upon the value of accepting children's feelings—all their feelings. He described how to avoid self-defeating patterns like sarcasm, warnings, and promises. At the conclusion of his talk, Dr. Ginott was surrounded by a group of parents who wanted to speak to him personally.

We decided not to push into the crowd. Instead we walked out into the cold night air, got into the car, and sat silently while the motor warmed up. We both knew that we had come upon something that had moved us deeply, and yet we couldn't identify what it was. We had heard things this evening that seemed simple enough to be immediately useful, and yet we sensed that these simple statements were based upon an idea so complex as to be limitless in its possibilities.

On the way home we tried to sort out our thoughts:

Would we be able to apply what we had learned tonight?

Would it work?

Wouldn't it be strange to say things in new ways?

How would the kids respond?

Would they even notice the difference?

Was it too late to make changes now?

Had permanent damage already been done?

How would we describe the whole thing to our husbands?

I thought about my explosion over the fingerpaints this morning. "Helen, I think I could have avoided that whole scene if I had only said, 'I see fingerpaints on the floor. We need some rags.' "

Helen looked at me and shook her head. "I'm unconvinced. You were pretty angry this morning. You don't sound very angry to me now. Dr. Ginott said, 'If you feel it, show it.' "

"All right," I said, "How's this? . . . 'When I see fingerpaints on the floor, I get so furious I feel like taking every jar of paint and throwing it in the garbage can!' "

"I'm very impressed," Helen said, "But will it work with real, live children? Hey! I just had a horrible thought. Suppose they never spill anything again!" We laughed as we realized that we were actually looking forward to the next mishap, hoping that it would come soon while we were still fresh.

We didn't have long to wait. The sun rose; the sun set. The milk spilled. We described. They mopped! It was a little miracle.

Astounded by our success, even if it was beginner's luck, we had to learn more. We bought Dr. Ginott's book, *Between Parent and Child,* and were delighted to find that it was rich in practical suggestions that could be used at once. Just seeing the words in print and being able to read certain portions of it over and over again, gave us something to hang on to.

There was the time, for example, I was about to go out for the evening when my youngest son, Andy, grabbed my leg crying, "Don't go, Mommy; stay home!" I gently pried him loose, picked up the book from the night table, locked myself in the bathroom, found the section headed "Parents do not need an entertainment license," and read at breakneck speed. When I came out, I was prepared. I said, "Honey, I know you wish we weren't going out tonight. You wish we would stay with you . . . but your father and I are going to enjoy a movie." It may have been a rote recitation, but it did get us out to the movies without the usual scene.

We found the chapter on praise useful. Formerly Helen had complimented five-year-old Billy with, "You're great, wonderful, the best!" She had never understood why he usually protested, "No, I'm not. Jimmy is better." Or, "Stop bragging about me." So she tried Dr. Ginott's prescription for praise. The day Billy fixed her stopped-up kitchen sink, she resisted saying, "Fantastic! You're a genius!" Instead she described what she felt and what she saw: "There I was, all upset, thinking I would have to call the plumber. Then you came in with a toilet plunger and in two minutes the stopped-up water went down. How did you ever think of it?" And then from a little child came the sweetest praise of all—the praise he conferred upon himself. "I used my brain," he said. "I'm a good plumber."

A mailing from our local child-guidance association announced that Dr. Ginott was starting a parent study group in our community. An application was enclosed for those who might be interested in joining. We both mailed ours back immediately.

Helen and I were pleased by the diversity of the group that met that first day. The women ranged in age from twenty-three to fifty. The size of their families varied, too—from one child to a brood of six. Most of the women were married, one was divorced, and one was widowed. We numbered amongst us housewives, teachers, businesswomen, an artist, and a musician. Our religious backgrounds differed as well. There were Protestants, Catholics, Jews, and atheists.

What we all had in common was children.

In the beginning the meetings took the form of lectures, and each lecture taught us new skills. We learned about the limits of logic in dealing with a child, and about the power of speaking to his emotions. We saw how it was possible to give a child in fantasy what we could not give him in reality.

For me, who had been so dedicated to the rational approach, this insight came as a gift. I can still hear the sound of my own voice as I sat in the car, patiently explaining to a grumpy David that we were *all* thirsty, that we couldn't *help* being stuck in traffic, that there was no way for us to stop and get a drink, that complaining wouldn't make the car go faster. . . .

What a relief it was now to be able to turn to my son in this same situation and say, "Hey, I hear a boy with a big thirst. I bet you wish you had a bucketful of ice-cold apple juice right now!"

When David broke into a smile and said, "How about a bathtubful!" I felt grateful for my new knowledge.

Another technique that made a difference in the tenor of the household was the ability to turn a threat into a choice: "If you use that water gun in the living room once more, you'll be sorry!" now became, "The water gun is not to be used in the living room. You may play with it in the bathroom or out of doors. You decide."

We also began to notice certain changes were taking place in ourselves. For one thing, we realized that we were talking less to our children. Apparently Dr. Ginott's oft-repeated dictum was having an effect upon us: "Whenever possible, replace a paragraph with a sentence, a sentence with a word, a word with a gesture." As we spoke less, we found ourselves listening more—and in a different way. We began to hear, behind the words, what a child was really saying. Andy's belligerent, "You're always taking David places—the library, the dentist, the Cub Scouts," I now heard as, "My brother is taking too much of your attention. I'm worried."

So I eliminated the long explanation and spoke to Andy's real concern: "Would you like me to spend more time with you? . . . I'd enjoy that, too."

We also found ourselves developing a certain emotional distance from our children. We were less easily affected by their foul moods, their Sturm und Drang. For Helen, who often felt she was living at a battlefront, her new ability to remain uninvolved was a boon. Now, instead of rushing forth to take up arms for one side or another, she remained calm and issued the kind of directions that could lead to a peaceful settlement. When her children began fighting over the use of the swing she was able to say, "Children, I have confidence that you can work out a solution that is fair to each of you." But the real triumph came five minutes later when a little voice called from the backyard, "Mommy, we decided. We're gonna take turns."

Not all of our stories had such happy endings. Enough occurred on the debit side to keep us from getting smug. The fact is, this new language wasn't really part of us yet. The words Helen used, and others like them, still felt alien to our tongues and awkward to our ears.

The children, too, seemed a little disconcerted by the new sounds. Every once in a while they stared up at us with a "Who-is-that-lady?" expression on their faces—and there were times when even we weren't sure who "that lady" was.

Our husbands regarded us with some suspicion, too. One didn't need a degree in psychology to identify the hostility in a statement like, "Okay, Mother, you're the expert. *You* take care of his temper tantrum." Or, "Since everything I say seems to be wrong, maybe you ought to write me a script."

And sometimes we behaved like the proverbial cow that gave good milk and then kicked over the pail. We said all the right things and then, unable to resist, added just one more sentence ("You'll get over it soon." Or, "In life you have to learn to take the bitter with the sweet.") and undid all our good work.

We were also plagued by the natural tendency to overdo each new skill. When we first discovered the extraordinary power of "That makes me furious!" we were thrilled. It felt so good to say it, and the children almost always hopped to attention and made amends. It was on the day I shouted, "I'm furious!" and got my first "Tough on you!" that I was clued in to the fact that I had been pushing a good thing too far.

Helen's fascination with the idea of fantasy fulfillment led her to intone, "Ah, you wish you had. . . ." so often to her seven-year-old daughter that one day Laurie wailed, "Mommy, there you go again!"

When Helen mentioned this to Dr. Ginott, he answered, "Some of these expressions are potent and must be used sparingly. Like strong seasoning the right amount adds flavor. Too much can make food indigestible."

Our course of study was drawing to a close, but our problems were not. There were periods when the children functioned beautifully—did well in school, made friends, contentedly explored their world, and were a pleasure to live with. But these sunny intervals were almost always followed by a series of storms that blew up from nowhere and without warning. (He's been attacked by other children at the bus stop. . . . He refuses to go to school in the morning. . . . He's started to wet his bed.) And sometimes the very skills we had learned to depend upon became a source of frustration because they kept leading us to new questions, which in turn demanded new answers.

"If I permit him to express all his feelings, and he tells me that he hates his little brother, what do I do then, Dr. Ginott?"

Maybe we needed another series of sessions. Dr. Ginott agreed to continue. In the sessions that followed, there were two new developments. First were the signs of change in our children. New sounds were in the air. Helen reported overhearing her daughter tell a friend, "In our house we don't blame each other." And I'll never forget the time my oldest son, David, stormed into his brother's room, yelled, "I'm so mad, I feel like punching your head in—but I won't!" and then stormed out again. To an outsider, this may not seem like progress, but in my house it was a miracle of self-restraint and one less bloody nose.

The second new element was our sense of freedom. For a long time now we had been concerned with our loss of spontaneity. Would we go through the rest of our lives weighing each word—worrying about the impact of each sentence? Intellectually, we understood that the mastery of any new skill involved a temporary giving up of spontaneity. Even a Horowitz must impose upon himself exercise, drill, and strict adherence to form before he can bring his own meaning to the music.

But still we fretted. It was so hard not to be spontaneous in this most near and dear of relationships. And so we were greatly relieved to find that suddenly we were feeling more natural, more comfortable. We took chances, improvised, experimented. We no longer sounded like each other or like Dr. Ginott. True, we were all using the same basic skills—but now we were bringing our own meaning to the music.

Then these sessions ended. Time out for a summer vacation, but with the promise that the group would be meeting again in the fall.

Summer came and went—and with it went a lot of our hard-won expertise. A whole summer with kids, kids, kids had done us in. We, who had been making music in June, were reduced to a few sour notes by September. We became aware that life with children, no matter how skilled the parents nor how enchanting the child, was an exhausting and confusing job with built-in hardships and conflicting needs. The children were noisy when we wanted quiet; they demanded attention when we needed time to ourselves; they were sloppy when we craved order. And the teasing, and the bickering, and the big deals made over little issues: "I don't want to brush my teeth!" "Why do I have to get into pajamas?" "I don't need a sweater."

Under the constant abrasiveness we found ourselves slipping back into old ways. The glow of the early successes was slowly fading. We were out of practice.

Dr. Ginott had often said that this approach was like learning a new language—French or Chinese. We realized now that we were doing something even harder. Along with learning this new language, we were "unlearning" a lifetime of another kind of speech, one that had been handed down to us from generations past.

Such phrases as:

Why can't you ever. . . .

You'll always be a. . . .

You never. . . .

Who did that?

What's the matter with you?

were like evil weeds that would not be rooted out. They had a fiendish way of reasserting themselves and strangling the tender new growth of:

You wish. . . .

I have confidence that you'll. . . .

Then you really feel that. . . .

It would be helpful if. . . .

So it was with mixed feelings that we returned in September —a little skeptical but still hopeful that at least some of our original enthusiasm would be restored. When the session began, we realized that we had not been alone in our feelings. Other voices echoed our sentiments. We heard "Boy, did I slip back this summer," and "I think I forgot everything I ever learned."

Dr. Ginott listened quietly to these comments, and then posed this question: What is our major goal as parents?

Someone ventured, "To improve parent-child relationships."

Another said, "To find better ways of communicating with our children."

Still another woman glibly said, "To produce children who are, among other things, brilliant, polite, charming, neat and well-adjusted, of course."

Dr. Ginott looked solemn. It was obvious that this last comment had not amused him. He leaned forward and said, "This is how I see it. It seems to me that our large goal is to find the ways to help our children become humane and strong.

"For what does it profit us if we have a neat, polite, charming youngster who could watch people suffer and not be moved to take action?

"What have we accomplished if we have reared a child who is brilliant—at the top of his class—but who uses his intellect to manipulate others?

"And do we really want children so well-adjusted that they adjust to an unjust situation? The Germans adjusted only too well to the orders of the Nazis to exterminate millions of their fellow men.

"Understand me: I'm not opposed to a child being polite or neat or learned. The crucial question for me is: What methods have been used to accomplish these ends? If the methods used are insults, attacks, and threats, then we can be very sure that we have also taught this child to insult, to attack, to threaten, and to comply when threatened.

"If, on the other hand, we use methods that are humane, then we've taught something much more important than a series of isolated virtues. We've shown the child how to be a person—a *mensch*, a human being who can conduct his life with strength and dignity."

From across the room Helen's eyes caught mine. There it was. That elusive idea that had so moved us at that first meeting had finally been identified. It was the concept of a process for humanizing—a concept that told us that every act of relating to a child had meaning, counted for something, became part of the fabric of the person he was to become. I could begin to see that when we said to a child, "The milk spilled" and handed him a sponge, we were doing more than using a clever technique for handling a minor mishap. On a much deeper level we were saying, "I see you as a person who is capable of helping himself."

We were telling him:

"In time of trouble we don't blame."

"In time of trouble we focus on solutions."

"In time of trouble we lend each other a helping hand."

All at once it became sharply clear to me that if the very process one uses with a child determines the kind of human being he becomes, then I could never again feel the same about my job as a parent. True, the daily irritations would still be there, but I saw them now as opportunities—opportunities to forge our children's character, opportunities to affirm the values I believed in.

The woman who had given the glib answer earlier spoke again. "I didn't realize I was doing such important work."

Dr. Ginott smiled, "It all depends upon how you look at it. Let me tell you a story:

"Three laborers were approached by a villager. 'What are you doing?' he asked them.

"The first worker said, 'I'm earning my living.'

"The second one said, 'I'm laying bricks.'

"The third one answered, 'I'm building a cathedral.'"

Silence. The woman nodded soberly.

I thought, "We too are laborers. Our work is raising children. Our bricks—our moment-by-moment responses. Our cathedral—the realization of our children's full humanity.

CHILDREN ARE PEOPLE

Chapter II
They Feel What They Feel

From the outset, Dr. Ginott was intent upon communicating to us the importance of accepting children's feelings. In a variety of ways he would reiterate his convictions:

All feelings are permitted; actions are limited.

We must not deny a child's perceptions.

Only after a child feels right, can he think right.

Only after a child feels right, can he do right.

I wasn't even sure I completely understood these ideas. Was it really that important to accept children's feelings? And if so, what did this have to do with making children humane and strong?

In my own past, a child's feelings seemed to count for very little. "She's only a kid; what does she know? The way she carries on, you'd think the world was coming to an end." As a youngster, I got the distinct impression that my feelings were not to be taken seriously until I reached maturity. I was accustomed to hearing:

"It's foolish to feel that way."

23

"You have no reason to be so upset."

"You're making a big fuss over nothing."

I never thought twice about it. That was the way it was. Yet now, as a parent, I was being told that my job was to help my children recognize their real feelings, because it was beneficial for them to know what they felt.

"You seem pleased at having finished that puzzle by yourself."

"You must be disappointed that Tommy couldn't come to your party."

We were also told that all of our children's feelings, even the negative ones, were to be acknowledged:

"A toy that's so hard to work can be frustrating."

"You really hate it when Aunt Harriet pinches your cheek."

I could see where holding up a mirror to feelings had merit. In some ways it did make for smoother family relations, to acknowledge a feeling rather than fight it. This morning at breakfast, when David said, "Yick, this egg is too loose!", I eliminated a long monologue about how he couldn't possibly know what he was talking about. I did not remind him that the egg was boiled exactly as long as the one he had eaten and enjoyed the day before. I simply said, "Oh, you like it firmer." This was a lot easier and kept the "egg issue" from boiling over into a mess of bad tempers.

But I still didn't understand the big mystique about feelings. Then something happened that gave me an insight into the whole process.

One stormy night during supper there was a crash of thunder and the house was plunged into total blackness. When the lights came on a few seconds later, the children seemed frightened. I thought the best way to handle it was to make light of their fears. I nearly tossed off, "There, that wasn't so bad, was it?" but my husband, Ted, spoke first. He said, "Hey, that was pretty scary." The children stared at him.

It sounded nice, his saying that. I caught his spirit. "It's funny," I said, "when a light is on in a room, everything feels so friendly and familiar. But take that same room with the same things in it and put it in darkness, and suddenly it becomes scary. I don't know why. It just does."

Six eyes looked up at me with such relief, such gratitude, that I was overwhelmed. I had made a very simple statement about a very ordinary event, and yet it seemed to mean so much to them. They began to talk, all at once, fighting each other for a turn.

DAVID: Sometimes I think a robber is going to come and kidnap me.

ANDY: My rocking chair looks like a monster in the dark.

JILL: What scares me like anything is when the tree branches scrape against the window.

The words spilled out, each child saying aloud the fearful thoughts he had had when alone in his dark room. We both listened and nodded. They talked and talked. Finally, they were done.

In the silence that followed, we all felt so loved and loving that I knew we must have touched the heart of a very powerful process. It was no small matter, this business of validating a child's feelings. Did other people know about it?

I began to eavesdrop on conversations between parents and children. At the zoo I heard:

CHILD: (*Crying*) My finger! My finger hurts!
FATHER: It couldn't hurt. It's only a little scratch.

At the supermarket I heard:

CHILD: I'm hot.

MOTHER: "How can you feel hot; it's cool in here.

In the toy store I heard:

CHILD: Mommy, look at this little duck. Isn't he cute?

MOTHER: Oh, that's for a little baby. You're not interested in baby toys any more.

It was astonishing. These parents seemed unable to hear their children's simplest emotions. Certainly they meant no harm by their responses. Yet, in reality, what they were telling their children, over and over again, was:

You don't mean what you say.

You don't know what you know.

You don't feel what you feel.

I had to contain myself not to tap each one of these parents on the shoulder and suggest that he say instead:

I see you have a scratch. A scratch can hurt.

or

It's really hot for you in here, isn't it?

or

Ah! You like that furry little duck, don't you?

I was bursting. If I couldn't tell strangers, at least I could tell friends. I had to spread the gospel. I called a few old friends whom I thought could put up with my fervor and described my recent revelations. They listened politely, even with interest. Then came the barrage of "buts."

"But Janet, I'm not even sure I understand what you mean when you say, 'Accept feelings; limit actions.' How would I apply it to Timmy?"

I thought of a few examples:

"Timmy, I know you'd like to gather up a big bunch of

these daffodils and bring them home. The sign says that flowers are not to be picked in the park."

"Timmy, I can see where you'd like to bite into every chocolate in the box just to see what's inside. It's very tempting. What you *may* do is to choose one piece now and another tomorrow."

"Timmy, you're so mad at Eric for breaking your bicycle, I bet you'd like to sock him. I know. But tell him with words, not with fists."

Another friend said, "But Janet, if you accept a child's feelings, aren't you really giving approval to them? My daughter won't let anyone come near her toys. Now I certainly don't want to validate that selfish feeling. I think it's important that Nancy grow up to be generous, so I teach her that we all have to learn to share."

And from still another friend I heard, "But Jan, if I let Roger tell me how much he hates the baby, won't I just be encouraging his worst feelings—reinforcing them—giving him permission to hate?"

It was so hard to explain. I tried to tell them that helping a child clarify his feelings didn't mean agreeing with the feelings or reinforcing them; that I wasn't talking about an approving response like, "Great Nancy, you hate to share!" Or "Marvelous Roger, you'd like to strangle your sister."

That I meant the kind of listening to and responding that comes from a real effort to "feel into" the children's emotions.

That your honest, simple "Oh" or "I see" tells your child, "Your feelings, *all* of them, are important—the good and bad. They are all part of you. Your feelings don't shock or frighten me."

That it isn't until a child's angry, hurting feelings are out in the open, until they are heard and accepted, that he is free to change.

I wasn't sure my unsolicited zeal was appreciated, so I was doubly pleased to receive two phone calls a few days later.

"Jan, the impossible just happened. Nancy's friend was at the house this morning and demanded that I make Nancy share her new Tinker toy. For the first time I thought about how Nancy might feel. And a strange thing happened. Instead of being angry with Nancy, I found myself feeling almost tender. I said, 'It seems to me that it must be very hard to share a new toy. People like to have new things to themselves for a long time.' Then to Nancy's friend I said, 'When Nancy is ready, then she'll share.' Nobody said a word, but a half hour later, I actually heard Nancy announce, 'Okay Barbara, I'm ready to share now!' "

My second caller had the same awed sound. "You won't believe this, Janet. This morning the baby was sleeping and Roger kept running in to pull her blanket off. I was about to whack him and say, 'You're a big boy now—you should know better!' But I remembered what you told me the other day about good feelings not flowing in until the bad ones have emptied out. So I just restrained his hand and said, 'Hey, Roddy, I've been thinking about how the baby must bother you sometimes. Even when she's sleeping. I'll bet that just having her in the house, just seeing her, can sometimes make you mad.' He gave me a long, grateful look and said, 'Baby's cold. Cover her.' Can you believe it?"

I was elated by these stories. They told me I was on the right track. Just accepting a feeling was enough to make a difference; and what a difference! Instead of irritated parents trying to impose their adult views upon balky children, here were parents who had really tried to listen and understand— here were children who had been heard, and who had felt understood—children who had been freed to respond more lovingly.

Then something happened that gave me pause. Mary Sue, Jill's best friend from nursery school days on, began to make fun of Jill—teasing her for wearing babyish clothes, whispering about her to other giggling girls. But Jill was so trusting of her old friend that she seemed unaware of what was happening. On Saturday, Jill telephoned Mary Sue to come over to play. This time Mary Sue lowered the boom. She told Jill that she didn't want to be her friend anymore, and that the other girls didn't like her, either.

Jill stood there stunned, devastated. Then she hung up the phone and went to her room. An hour later I passed by her open door and saw her lying on her bed with a tearstained face, staring at the ceiling. Suddenly all I wanted to do was get my hands on that Mary Sue and shake her till her teeth rattled. That mean, self-centered brat—how dare she do that to Jill? I wanted to tell my child that the dirt under her fingernail was worth more than all of Mary Sue put together. I wanted to shout, "And the apple doesn't fall far from the tree! Just look at the mother—that cold, hypocritical peacock!" But most of all, I wished for the power to ease Jill's suffering, for the words of wisdom that could help her.

What kind of advice could I give her? I knew that children usually didn't appreciate advice. I also knew that Jill needed time to work through her own solutions. And yet I felt driven to solve her problem. Empathy in this case seemed out of the question. I was afraid that if I were to mirror back her pain, her rejection, her loneliness, that she would become completely undone.

In my gentlest tone I said, "Honey, you can't go through life depending upon just one friend. You're such a wonderful girl. You could have lots of friends. Why don't you call someone else to play with today?"

Jill burst into tears and cried, "You're always telling me

what to do! What makes you think I wasn't going to? Well, I'm not *now!*"

I brooded over this incident all day. If offering a solution wasn't the answer, what was? What could I have done to help my child? I couldn't be expected to merely empathize and then sit back and watch her suffer.

There seemed to be a built-in limitation to this tender theory of accepting our children's feelings. Certainly it worked for the small troubles; the scratched finger, the lost toy, the disappointment over a rained-out picnic. But what about the big hurts—real loss; the death of a beloved pet, rejection by a friend? Would it be appropriate, or even helpful, to play back these feelings? Would I not be doing more harm than good by opening these wounds?

I brought my doubts to our next session. Dr. Ginott shook his head. "I wish I knew the way," he said, "to convince parents that suffering can promote growth, that struggle can strengthen character. Parents so want their children to be happy that often they deprive them of the maturing experiences of disappointment, frustration, and grief. 'Don't cry,' they say, 'we'll get you another dog.'

"If parents could only believe that they strengthen their children when they identify painful emotions, they would not be afraid to say, 'You miss Prince. You feel as if your heart would break. . . . I know, I know.' *This* is actually the finest help we can give our children.

"When your child gets a cut, nothing on earth can heal the wound immediately. You apply antiseptic and a Band-Aid and know that time will do the rest. For wounds of the spirit, it is the same. We give emotional first-aid, but we must understand that the healing process itself is slow. We can say to Jill, 'To have a best friend turn away from you after so many years hurts. It hurts a lot. It can also make a person suddenly feel very lonely.'

"Then Jill can say to herself, 'I may have lost a friend, but I have a mother who understands.' "

I went home a little dazed by what I had heard. I had never thought about any of these things before: the place for genuine suffering in a child's life. . . . The power, the extraordinary power of a parent to give solace simply by understanding the depths of the emotions. . . . A parent—not destroyed by the child's grief, not denying it—but strong, hearing the anguish, knowing the pain, and giving his child by the very act of his listening, the most profound message of all: *It can be endured.* As long as one person in the world can really hear us, really feel with us; it can be endured.

I was lost in these thoughts when the door slammed. I looked up and saw six-year-old Andy standing in the middle of the room, his face contorted.

"The teacher yelled at me," he said hoarsely. "I was picking up my pencil from the floor, and she started to yell. She said I wasn't paying attention. Everybody was looking at me. She said I had to stay after school and that would teach me a lesson. She made me stay. And you didn't know where I was!"

My heart fell. How awful it must have been for him. Quick, quick, I'd brush away the hurt, say it was nothing, nothing to be upset about. I'd tell him to try to pay more attention in the future. A kiss, a cookie, and he'd be fine, just fine!

Then I remembered a long time ago another little child in the first grade made to stand in the corner for talking. I remembered the cracked paint of that dim corner and the shuffling sounds of the children filing past as they went home for lunch. And the terrible quiet. Then the sudden, sharp voice, "You can go home now, Janet. I hope you learned your lesson."

I remember running all the way home, wanting to shout, wanting to scream, wanting to cry, wanting most of all to tell my mother. "Don't talk so much," she kept saying. "Eat. You'll be late." And I remembered chewing and trying to swallow the dry sandwich.

I pulled Andy onto my lap. "That can be very upsetting, having a teacher yell at you." He flung his arms around my neck and buried his head in my shoulder. "And having the whole class look at you! That can make it twice as bad. Then to have to sit there all that time after everyone else had gone home, wanting all the while to run home yourself and not being able to. What a bunch of mean, hurting feelings to have all at once!"

I had been so intent on trying to reach out to the truth of Andy's experience and so involved with consoling my sobbing child that I was startled to find that tears had been streaming down my own cheeks, and that I was suddenly flooded with a strange sense of relief.

I don't know how long we sat there, rocking quietly. I only know when it was all over that somehow I had reached back across thirty years and taken a little girl out of the corner.

Chapter III
Feelings and Variations

For a long time we were sure that just listening to and validating a child's feelings was the main theme of a humane relationship. And basically it was. But we eventually discovered that this theme had many variations and it was useful to know them all.

VARIATION I

Some children had a need to be heard that went beyond their parents' listening endurance. A way had to be found to terminate the talk and still let the children know that we cared.

Lee reported that she listened to her daughter, Susie, complain for ten minutes about not getting a part in the school play.

"I tried to comfort her," she said, "but Susie kept raving on. It was more than I could take. I thought to myself, 'It's time to summarize and call a halt.'

"Susie," I said, "I hear you. You've been telling me that you wanted a part very badly. You felt you were just as good as anybody else who tried out for it—maybe better. I understand, but I can't listen any more. I'm going into the kitchen now, and while I'm preparing supper, I'll be knowing how disappointed and angry you are."

VARIATION II

Sometimes the children expressed their feelings in language that was so offensive that we couldn't listen—much less help. We each had a different level of tolerance, but certain statements got to us all.

"Daddy looks like an old man. Why do I have to have such an old Daddy?"

"My teacher is a stupid ass."

When Laurie said to Helen, "I hope you die," Helen retorted, "That's unacceptable! I can see you're angry, but you'll have to find another way to tell me about it. And now, I'd like to be alone for the next hour." To Laurie's, "Why?" she simply answered, "You think about it!"

VARIATION III

Sometimes a small offering would help a child in distress. We never asked whether he wanted it or not, we just gave it. A new crayon, a balloon, a box of raisins at the right time would speak directly to his heart.

When Roslyn's five-year-old son tearfully complained, "Mommy likes everybody better than me," she put her arm around him and said, "Are you feeling unloved? That's not a pleasant feeling to have—not at all. I think this is a good time for a hug and hot chocolate."

When Lee's son had hysterics over a microscopic bruise inflicted by his brother in a wrestling match, Lee took two pieces of ice, wrapped them in a red wash cloth, and gave it to him to apply to his "wounded" arm.

VARIATION IV

When a child was in the grip of a powerful emotion, we were sometimes able to help him channel his feelings into a creative outlet. Dr. Ginott had said that there should be a redundancy of creative material in the home—pens, pencils, crayons, paint, pads, cardboard, blackboards, boxes, clay, and so forth. The women in our group had taken him literally. Hardly a week went by that we didn't hear about a poem written to express grief over the death of a pet turtle; a letter written to a TV station to protest a favorite program going off the air; or an angry picture drawn of the bully on the block.

For the child who was either too young or who chose not to draw or write, a parent could act as secretary.

Evelyn's seven-year-old son, Stevie, came home one afternoon from day camp in a rage. His counselor had said that unless he went down the ten-foot slide at the deep end of the pool, he'd be taken out of his swimming group and would have to use the kiddy pool.

As Stevie ranted on, his father quietly picked up a pen and began to write. When Stevie stopped for breath, father said, "Boy, you must have been pretty mad at your counselor today. Listen to what you've been saying: "That big shot thinks he's the boss over everybody. He's so mean, I hate him.' "

Stevie listened enthralled. "Yeah," he said earnestly, "and put down that I'm going to push him off the slide and hold his head under until he drowns."

Father wrote as fast as he could.

"Now write that I'll pull the plug out of the pool, and all the water will go out of the hole and he'll go down too."

That sentiment was also added to the list. When his whole speech was read back to him, Stevie nodded vigorously and asked to hear it again.

"Here," said his father handing him the paper. "You can keep it and read it to yourself whenever you like. Now *I* have a letter to write. Please deliver it to your counselor tomorrow. It will say: 'My son, Steven, is not—under any circumstances whatsoever—to go on the ten-foot slide until *he* feels that he is ready."

VARIATION V

There is a time and place for *not* understanding, for *not* being in touch, for *not* knowing what a child is feeling. Dr. Ginott describes this as "letting each child have a corner on his own soul."

I can still remember Jill when she was four, lying on the bed, sucking her finger and staring at me.

"Do you know what I'm thinking?" she asked.

"No," I answered.

"It's a good thing," she said, and popped her finger back in her mouth.

VARIATION VI

There is a place in a child's life for the trumpet sound that summons up his courage—his fighting spirit. We call it "the bracing message." It's not the usual statement that parents make when they think they are strengthening their children, giving them armor to face the harsh realities of the outside world. It's not the cold, impersonal "Tough kid; you'll survive," but the compassionate acknowledgment, "Yes, it *is* tough. Yes, it *is* hard. I respect your struggle and have faith that you'll find a way."

For example, Helen said to Laurie, "Even though your teacher is sarcastic to you, you're still learning from her—despite her unpleasant manner!"

And Ted said to Andy, "I saw how you ignored that kid who teased you about not being taller. I guess you know that in this family what we value in a person is not his size, but his character."

But the example that moves me the most concerns Nell, who had lost her husband several months ago. In one of our sessions she poured out problem after problem for which there seemed to be no answer. Her son was miserable about being fatherless. He complained constantly, even blaming her for his plight. She felt hopeless.

In the heavy silence that followed, we waited for Dr. Ginott to apply the balm of empathy. We were startled when he looked at her with great intensity and said, "Nell, don't let life defeat you."

Her eyes filled with tears and someone discreetly changed the subject.

The next week there was a new look about Nell. Helen

asked her how things were going. "I'm not sure," she said, "but something is different. The next time Kenneth started to complain, I stopped him. I said, 'Kenneth, I know it hasn't been easy for you since Dad died. We're a one-parent family now and we wish it were otherwise. But I think it's time for both of us to start thinking about how to be the best one-parent family we can be!' "

That afternoon, without a word to his mother, Kenneth mowed the long-neglected lawn.

Chapter IV
When a Child Trusts Himself

As the weeks went by, and I became more aware of the role that feelings played in my children's lives, I came to a number of realizations that were very new to me.

A FEELING IS A FACT

My children's feelings had become as real to me as apples, pears, chairs, or any other physical object. I could no more ignore what the children felt than I could ignore a barricade in the middle of the road. It is true that their feelings could change—sometimes very quickly—but while these feelings were being felt there was no greater reality.

It was not unusual to hear:

"Why do you stick up for Andy? You always take his side."

Or, "We never go anyplace; everybody else does."

At one time I would have met this kind of nonsense head-on with the full strength of my adult logic.

"That's not true. I take your side plenty of times and you know it."

Or, "How can you say that? Didn't we just go to the zoo last week? You have a short memory."

Now I received a different inner message from these statements. *If a child is feeling a certain way, that's the way it really is for him at that moment.* Realizing this, I was able to formulate another kind of answer.

"To you it seems that I take Andy's part all the time? I see. Thank you for sharing your feelings with me."

Or, "As far as you're concerned, this family doesn't go on enough trips. You'd like us to go places together a lot more often. I'm glad you told me about it. Now I know."

TWO OR MORE CONTRADICTORY FEELINGS CAN EXIST SIDE BY SIDE

When I internalized this thought, certain kinds of statements became obsolete:

"Well, *do* you miss her or *don't* you?"

"Make up your mind, you either want to go to camp or you don't."

Now I sensed another truth—the truth of:

"In one way you miss your friend, and in another way you're glad she's moved away."

"One part of you wants to go back to your old camp, another part wants to stay home, and still another part wants to try a new camp."

EACH CHILD'S FEELINGS ARE UNIQUE

As no two leaves on the same tree are exactly alike, so no two children feel exactly the same way about the same things.

And it was this very difference that we came to appreciate—the difference that made him "him", and nobody else.

I could no longer say with annoyance, "How come you don't like ice cream? You're the only one in the family who doesn't." Now I could observe his "difference" with pleasure. Even his dislike was a mark of distinction: "Your brother loves ice cream. It doesn't appeal to you at all. You prefer ices."

I tried to give the message that differences weren't liabilities. I focused instead on strengths. I replaced "All the boys have joined Little League. Why do you have to be different?" with "Baseball is something you don't seem to especially enjoy. I notice you have other interests."

WHEN FEELINGS ARE IDENTIFIED AND ACCEPTED, CHILDREN BECOME MORE IN TOUCH WITH WHAT IT IS THEY FEEL

From David I heard: "When you talk to me that way, Dad, I feel accused; and then I feel I have to defend myself."

From Andy I heard: "Mommy, do you know why I'm acting this way? It's because I want to be noticed."

From Jill I heard: "I made a box to show how I feel at different times. I call it my mood box. It has pictures of when I'm angry, joyous, furious, happy, sad, and blah."

WHEN PARENTS RESPECT THEIR CHILDREN'S FEELINGS, THE CHILDREN IN TURN LEARN TO RESPECT AND TRUST THEIR OWN FEELINGS

This somewhat obvious observation was not always so obvious to me. It took a series of personal experiences for me to begin to understand how important it was to teach a child to trust his own perceptions.

The first incident took place when Ted and I were picking up Jill's bicycle at the repair shop. She was seven then. As soon as she spotted her bike, she wheeled it outside. Meanwhile Ted walked around to the front to pay the cashier. A moment later Jill was back with a troubled look on her face. "The brake isn't right," she said.

The mechanic looked annoyed. "There's nothing wrong with the brake. I worked on that bicycle myself."

Jill looked at me unhappily. "It doesn't feel right to me."

The mechanic was firm. "It's just a little stiff—that's all."

Jill said timidly, "No, it's not just stiff, it *feels* funny." Then she ran to tell her father.

It was an uncomfortable moment. The mechanic's look clearly indicated, "Lady, your kid is a pain in the neck. Don't tell me you're going to take her word over mine." I didn't know what to do. Here I had been trying to teach Jill that her inner voice was worth listening to, trying to teach her to say to herself, "If I'm feeling something, there may well be something to what I feel." On the other hand, here was a competent mechanic insisting that there was nothing wrong.

His scowl was too much for me. I mumbled something about how I was sure he was right, and that children do sometimes tend to exaggerate. At that moment Ted walked over and matter-of-factly said, "My daughter feels there's something wrong with the brake."

Sullenly, without a word, the mechanic lifted the bicycle onto a stand, examined the wheel, and said, "You'll have to leave it here. It needs a new section for the hub. The brakes are gone."

I was so affected by what had almost happened, that I vowed to myself "Never again!"

A few weeks later Jill and I were waiting for the light on a busy intersection. I took her by the hand and started to cross the street, but she pulled me back. I was about to let her know how annoyed I was, when I remembered. I said, "Jill, I'm glad to see you trust your own sense of timing, your own feeling of what's safe for you. We'll cross when it feels right to you and that will take as long as it has to take."

As we stood there shivering for five minutes while I saw ten opportunities to cross, I said to myself that anyone watching me would think I was crazy. Maybe I was overdoing this business of teaching her to respect her feelings.

Then an incident occurred which permanently changed my thinking. It was a hot summer afternoon. Jill came bursting into the house, her bathing suit still wet, a strange look on her face.

"We were having such a great time in the pool with this nice teen-age boy we met," she said. "He played water-tag with us. Then later he took Linda and me off to the side where the trees are. He asked me if he could lick my toes. He said it would be fun."

I hardly breathed. "And then what?" I said.

"I didn't know what to do. Linda thought it was funny, but I didn't want him to. It made me feel . . . I don't know."

I said, "You mean there was something about the whole thing that didn't seem right to you even though you didn't know what it was?"

"Yes," she nodded, "so I ran home."

I tried not to let her see my great relief. As casually as I could, I said, "You trusted your feelings, and they told you just what to do, didn't they?"

And then the enormity of it hit me. Could a child's trust in himself, in his own perceptions, help to keep him safe? And if we deny a child his perceptions, do we dull his ability to sense danger, and make him vulnerable to the influence of those who do not have his welfare at heart?

The outside world works hard to make a child deaf to his own warning bell:

"So what if there's no lifeguard. You know how to swim."

"There's no reason to be afraid. Even if a car comes, you have plenty of time to steer your sled out of the way."

"Don't be chicken. All the kids are trying it. It's not habit-forming."

Is it possible that sometimes a child's very survival will depend upon his trust in his own small inner voice?

A year ago, if someone had asked me about the significance of validating children's feelings, I would have answered feebly, "Well, I suppose it makes for less friction, and it certainly doesn't do any harm."

Now let the questioner beware; he will get a more passionate reply. For now I am strongly aware that when we tell a child that he doesn't feel what he is feeling, we strip him of his natural protection. Not only that. We confuse him, disorient him, desensitize him. We force him to construct a false world of words and defense mechanisms that have nothing to do with his inner reality. We separate him from who he is. And when we do not permit him to know what he feels, I suspect that he becomes less able to feel for others.

But oh, when we acknowledge the reality of a child's feelings, what splendid gifts do we bring: the strength to act upon his inner promptings . . . the possibility of a caring heart . . . the opportunity to be in touch with a unique human being—himself.

Chapter V

Letting Go:
A Dialogue on Autonomy

Helen had something on her mind. She telephoned to ask if she could come over for a while. As soon as she walked through the door I could see that she was agitated. She stood there with her coat on and launched into a long monologue.

"Jan, I don't know if you were aware of it, but I could hardly sit through that session yesterday. There was something about the discussion that made me so uneasy! I know this may sound a little paranoid, but I kept feeling that every word out of Dr. Ginott's mouth was being directed at me.

"I didn't react that way at first. When he said, 'One of our most important goals is to help our children separate from us,' I thought, 'That's self-evident. Nobody wants an overgrown child of thirty living in the house!' . . . But then, he went on to say, 'The measure of a good parent is what he is willing *not* to do for his child,' and I shriveled inside. 'Oh God,' I thought, 'if that's the measure of a good parent, I just don't measure up.' "

She paused for a moment and then continued speaking,

more to herself than to me. "On the other hand, if I do too much for my children, it's only because I really believe it's for their good. If Billy forgets his lunch and I don't bring it to school, he gets upset and goes hungry. He won't eat those school lunches. . . . If I don't drill Laurie before her spelling tests, she does very poorly and gets discouraged. If I don't drive the two of them to school in bad weather, they both catch cold; it never fails."

Suddenly she turned to me. "Now what am I doing that's so terrible? Isn't that what parents are for—to help and protect their children? Yet, after hearing Dr. Ginott say again and again 'we help most by not helping,' I'm not so sure anymore. Maybe what I'm doing isn't good for them."

Helen walked into the living room and I followed. "But who's to say he's right," she muttered. "The experts have been wrong before, you know! Oh maybe there are a few things I do for the children that they could be doing for themselves. Billy is seven now and he still comes into my room every morning and hands me his brush. He can brush his hair perfectly well himself, but when I get finished with him, he looks so handsome and appealing. . . . Now I can't believe that something as innocent as brushing a child's hair for him can make him less autonomous!

"Autonomous! I was in such a state after that last session I went to the dictionary to see if I still knew what the word meant. I guess I was hoping that the literal definition would somehow bail me out. That was a mistake. According to Webster, autonomous means self-regulating, self-governing, inner-directed and separate. That certainly does *not* describe my children. They're still asking me what to wear for school every day—and what's worse, I'm still telling them."

"Helen," I said, "you're being too hard on yourself!"

She ignored me. "A better description of my kids would be

'mother-regulated, mother-governed, and mother-directed.' As for 'separate,' when I think of that, I don't know whether to laugh or cry. Sometimes I feel so connected to them that I'm not sure where I leave off and they begin. Laurie gets 100 on a test, and I feel as if I got 100. Billy doesn't make the team, and I feel as if I didn't make the team."

Helen sank down heavily on the sofa. "It isn't as if I hadn't heard the principles of autonomy often enough. I just don't seem to be able to apply them. What is it that Dr. Ginott always says? 'The intellect can only absorb what the emotions will allow.' Well, evidently my emotions haven't been allowing very much to get through to my brain."

I sat down beside Helen. We both frowned and stared at the floor. I didn't know what to say. "Helen," I asked weakly, "should I get my notes? Think it would help?"

"Your notes!" she exclaimed. "You don't need notes. Why do you think I've come to *you?* It's because I've seen how easily you let your kids take over for themselves. I still remember that winter day Jill came home wearing nothing but gym shorts and a gym shirt. If it had been Laurie, I would have been frantic and demanded to know where her coat was. Not you. When Jill said, 'Mommy, the bus driver told me I'd "catch it" when I got home. What are you going to do to me?' I'll never forget your answer. Very quietly you said, 'On a cold day I expect *you* to be in charge of putting on your own coat!'

"And there's another incident that I'll never forget. It was the day David burst into the house shouting 'I forgot my violin again today. It's the third week in a row! You have to remind me from now on. It's every Tuesday.'

"Do you know what you did? You just nodded sympathetically and said something like, 'It's hard to remember these once-a-week lessons, isn't it, David? But I know you. Somehow or other, you'll figure out a way to remind yourself.'

"Do you know what I would have done? I would have made a big note for myself to remind *me* to remind *him* every Tuesday. The point I'm trying to make, Jan, is that you're a natural."

I listened to Helen with interest. Was it more natural for me? Why would it be? I tried to think back to how it was when I was a child. My parents were both immigrants—hardworking, busy; my mother forever cooking and cleaning; my father constantly preoccupied with trying to keep his small business going. It was hard for them just to feed and clothe us. They expected us to do the rest for ourselves.

And we did. We returned our own library books, took the subway or bus when we had to go somewhere, and worried our way through our own school problems. The only time we involved our parents in our school affairs was when we needed them to sign our report cards. Even then, the emphasis wasn't on our marks; it was on their signatures. I can still see my father clearing a space at the kitchen table, ceremoniously sitting down, and proudly and painstakingly writing out his full name—in English.

I guess my parents really did me a favor. They didn't set out to give me my autonomy. They probably wouldn't even have known what the word meant; but I got it anyway—by default.

I told Helen about some of this.

"Do you realize what a present they gave you?" she said. "My childhood was so different. I had to account to my mother for practically everything—my clothes, my grades, my whereabouts, my friends. I still remember coming home from a date, knowing that all the lights would be on and that both my parents would be waiting up for me. They couldn't sleep until I gave them the full report. Sometimes I think they enjoyed my dates more than I did."

"Boy, that must have been hard to take!"

"No, not really. I didn't know any other way. But I can see where your background gives you a distinct advantage. I get the whole picture now. You were given a lot of independence, and that's why it's so easy for you to pass it on to your children."

"Not so fast," I said. "Maybe my particular background helped, but the skills I use now didn't come from my parents. For instance, I always thought that every question deserved an answer. It would never have occurred to me *not* to answer a child's questions. It was only after Dr. Ginott talked about how a child needs air and room to explore his own thoughts, and how adults with their ready answers infringe upon a child's right to think, that I began to hold back.

"The first time I deliberately didn't answer a question felt very strange to me. One morning David asked, 'Do you think Jimmy and Tommy would get along with each other? They're both coming home with me today.' Well, that was the most provocative question anyone had put to me in days! I was all set to launch into a character analysis of the two boys, and to top it off with a prediction for the future of their relationship, when I suddenly remembered. I bit my tongue and said, 'That's an interesting question. What do *you* think, David?' He pondered awhile. Then he said, 'I think first they'll fight and then they'll be friends.' "

I thought Helen would smile at that. Instead she looked at me with such intensity that I felt compelled to go on.

"Do you remember the story Dr. Ginott told about a husband who wouldn't let his wife learn to drive. 'Sweetheart,' he said to her, 'there's no reason for you to have the headache of driving a car. As long as I'm around, just ask me and I'll be happy to take you any place you want to go.'

"I put myself in the wife's position and all at once I saw how frustrated children must feel when adults take over and don't let them do things for themselves. And I thought of the thousands of little ways that a parent can make his child feel helpless and dependent. But always in the name of 'love.'

"Mommy will unscrew the jar for you, dear."

"Here, let me button you up, sugar."

"Do you need any help with your homework?"

"I've laid out your clothes for you, honey."

"It always sounds so innocent, and the parent has the best of intentions, but it still adds up to one thing: You need Mommy. You can't manage by yourself."

"Now you'd think that this new insight would have inspired me to go right home and do everything differently. It didn't. I had to listen to example after example from the other women before I could even begin to make changes in my own home.

"Helen, did you know that I used to mastermind the children's departure every morning? How else could they assemble their lunches, books, sneakers, glasses, notes, money, mittens, and boots? *I* had to be there to hold coats, zip zippers, tie hoods, yank boots, and goad them on with reminders of the time.

"Then one morning, I made myself leave the room and called out, 'Let me know when you're ready to go, kids!' For ten minutes I sat on my bed like an obsolete piece of machinery. When they finally came clumping in to say goodbye, all bundled up and pleased with themselves, it suddenly seemed very unimportant that not all the buttons were buttoned, and that the big one was wearing the little one's mittens."

Helen continued to look at me with almost pained interest. I tried to think of another example. "I'll tell you something else that never would have happened if I hadn't consciously been using my new skills. David was eight when he told me that he needed money and that he wanted to get a job. It was

almost unbearable for me not to tell him—ever so kindly—
that no one would hire an eight-year-old. But that was the day
Dr. Ginott had thundered, '*Do not take away hope; do not
prepare for disappointment.*' So all I said was, 'I see.' The next
hour was hard to believe. David dragged out the phone books,
talked about the kind of work he thought he could do, looked
up the names of local merchants, made phone calls, and talked
to store managers. Finally, he told me, 'Did you know you
have to be fourteen and have working papers to get a job?
When I'm a teenager I'm going to work in the hardware store.
He's a nice man, the owner, and I like being around tools.'

"Helen, do you realize how close I came to butting in and
depriving him of that whole experience? My own mother
would have said, 'What kind of foolishness is this! Who lets
an eight-year-old look for work?' "

Helen winced. "Please, Jan, enough! I felt depressed before.
Now I could crawl into a hole."

It crossed my mind that I was being insufferable, but I was
too wound up to stop. "Helen, do you know what I enjoy most
of all? Not being a drill sergeant anymore. I used to rap out
orders all day long: 'Clear the blocks! Wash your hands! Put
on your rubbers! Shut the door!' It's such a pleasure now to be
able to describe a problem instead of barking a command. I
love singing out, 'Kids, the door's open!' or 'Weatherman says
rain today!' "

Helen got up and reached for her coat. "Jan, I can't listen
to you anymore. Do you hear yourself? 'Enjoyed,' 'a pleasure,'
'loved singing out.' Well, I don't sing out. It would be out of
character for me. It's not my style."

"Look," I said, a little miffed, "I don't want any medals,
but that 'style' you mention took some doing. Would it make
you feel better to hear about how stupid and discouraged I

felt along the way? Would you like to know, for instance, how at first I couldn't even manage as simple a thing as keeping quiet when someone asked my child a question?"

Helen sat down again.

"It happened last year. My Aunt Sophie came to visit and she asked Andy how old he was. I said to myself, 'I will *not* speak for him. It's important that a child have the opportunity to answer for himself.' But when I saw him staring up at her with his mouth open like the village idiot, I couldn't stand it. Before I knew it, I'd blurted out, 'six!' "

"I feel a little better," Helen said.

"It might also cheer you to know that some of the easiest principles were the hardest for me to accept. I almost resented it when Dr. Ginott talked about depending more upon other people to help us with our children. Do you remember him saying, 'Ask yourself: In this situation who can be most effective with my child—the salesman, the teacher, the dentist, the den mother?'

"I didn't go along with that at all. What outsider could match me for effectiveness with my own children? So you can imagine what a shock it was to discover that the most ordinary statement from the outside world—just because it *was* from the outside world—had an impact that I could never match.

"For example, I'd been doing verbal somersaults for over a month trying to get David to the barber. Nothing worked. Then one day he breezed in with 'Hey Ma, I gotta get a haircut this afternoon.' Helen, do you know who did it? It was the school custodian. Do you know what he said? He said, 'David, you need a haircut.'

"And I'll tell you something else that was hard for me— and that still is a battle. It's keeping my nose out of my children's business. I itch to question and comment about every little thing. Do you realize what I *don't* say when Jill comes home? I don't say, 'Did your teacher like your composition? What did she say about it? Was the math homework I helped you with all right? Your new dress looks so pretty on you. Did anyone notice it?'

"Do you know what restraint it takes just to say, 'Hi, Pumpkin,' and let her tell me anything *she* thinks is important?"

For the first time that afternoon Helen broke into a smile, "At last! You've finally mentioned the one thing I *don't* do to my children! I've had my mother's running commentary imposed on me for so long, and in such heavy doses, that I wouldn't have the heart to inflict it on my own kids.

"I still hear it every week with every visit: 'You look tired, dear. Are you getting enough rest? Does Jack always come home so late from work? Why do you wait till the last minute to take the roast beef out of the freezer? It will never be done on time. I don't mean to interfere dear, but I think meat tastes better when it's defrosted first.'

"When I hear that, Jan, I'm stopped in my tracks. Suddenly, I find myself explaining that I'm getting plenty of sleep, explaining that Jack is in his busy season now, defending the merits of cooking frozen meat, reassuring my mother that dinner will be served on time. . . .

"You know, Jan, just saying it out loud makes me see how disgusting it is. It's like telling your child, 'I must be part of everything that happens to you. I'd like to gnaw on every detail of your life. You couldn't manage without Mother's opinion, approval, guidance.' . . . And the worst part is that the constant comments and questions rob a child of time—time for his own experience to set, jell, and yield up its own meaning."

"That's right!" I exclaimed excitedly. Then I stared at her. Anyone who could express herself that eloquently probably knew a lot more than she thought she did.

"Helen," I said, "I have to shift gears. For a while you nearly had me convinced that you were an overbearing, over-protective mother. If I had stopped to think for a minute, I would have realized it wasn't so."

Helen looked bewildered.

"The time with Laurie and the Brownie poster contest," I prompted.

"Oh that," Helen said disparagingly.

"Yes, that! You had a dozen opportunities there to move in and take over. Laurie tried very hard to get you to make up her mind for her. She followed you from room to room asking, 'Mommy, what should I do? Should I enter the contest or shouldn't I? Do you think I could win?' . . . Do you remember how you answered her?"

Helen shook her head.

"You put the decision exactly where it belonged—in Laurie's lap. You said, 'You're thinking of entering a contest. That's exciting! And you're wondering whether you could win. . . . Laurie, what do *you* think?' She held her breath and said, 'I'm going to try.'

"And did you say, 'That's a wise decision dear. After all, nothing ventured, nothing gained.' No, you didn't. Instead you gave the most helpful response possible: You said, 'Oh.'

"But what really amazed me was what happened a few weeks later when Laurie came home with an honorable mention ribbon. I would have gushed, 'Laurie, you're wonderful. I'm so proud of you!' But you just hugged her and said, 'Laurie, you must be so proud of yourself!' And oh, the way she stood there—so tall, so full of herself.

"Now, damn it, any woman who can so clearly enjoy her

child's triumph without having to make it her own, knows a lot more than she's letting on."

Helen looked uncomfortable. "I was probably on good behavior because you were there. Okay, so I can put on a show for company, but you should see me when no one's around. Jan, I don't know why I'm the only one who has so much trouble with autonomy. I tell you it was pure torture yesterday to have to sit there at that session and listen to all those success stories.

"Did you hear Roslyn? She sounded perfectly relaxed about her daughter getting off late to school. She was so sure that one sharp scolding from the teacher would be more effective than her own daily nagging.

"I couldn't do that. I'd have to protect Laurie from her teacher's displeasure.

"And look at Lee. She refused to get into a fight with her kids when they played in the snow without their gloves. She told us she was confident that they would come in for their gloves when they were cold enough, and that she'd be happy to rub their hands or make them a hot drink.

"I'd have worried about frostbite.

"And Katherine—she found her son's lunchbox on the kitchen table and didn't feel obligated to dash off to school with it. I guess she figured that whatever happened—whether he borrowed money from his teacher, got half a sandwich from a friend, or even went hungry—he'd still be ahead of the game. He'd have had an experience that would tell him he could survive without Mommy.

"So you see, Jan, it's not that I don't know what I *should* be doing, it's just that I can't bring myself to do it. It goes against all my natural instincts—to help, to protect, to manage. . . . It's my problem."

I wanted to shake her. "The fact is, it's not your problem!

It's every parent's problem. You say giving autonomy isn't natural for you. I'll tell you what's natural for parents. It's natural to want to hold on, protect, control, advise, direct. It's natural to want to be needed, important, vital to our children.

"It's the other way that's not natural. Separating our children's hopes from ours, separating their disappointments from ours. Permitting them their struggle. Making ourselves dispensable. Letting go. That a parent can do it at all is a miracle."

Helen was silent for a long time. When she finally spoke, it was in a manner so halting and a voice so low, that I had to lean forward to hear her.

"I suppose you could say that giving autonomy is actually a way of giving love to your child. . . . It *is* more loving to let him use his own power to go on, isn't it? . . . It really *is* more loving to let him experience—even unpleasant things, isn't it? . . . You could almost say that any other way is hateful. It's like not letting him live."

Helen stood up suddenly and walked to the door.

"Where are you going?" I asked.

"Home," she said. "There's something I have to give my children."

"What's that?" I asked.

She turned and smiled. "Some healthy neglect," she said.

Chapter VI

"Good" Isn't Good Enough:
A New Way to Praise

Roslyn, an open, earnest young mother, started our next session. In lively detail she described a chance meeting with her old college roommate.

"I took one look at her and did the strangest thing. I pretended I didn't recognize her. I don't know why. She was always nice enough. But somehow, she had a way of making me feel so . . . unsure of myself . . . not quite bright.

"For a moment I considered walking in the other direction, and then I thought to myself, 'This is ridiculous! I'm a grown woman now. I have a family.'

" 'Hello Marcia!' I called, as if I'd just discovered her. 'After all these years!'

"She was so happy to see me that I felt like a rat for trying to avoid her. She flung her arms around me and said, 'Roslyn do you live near here? I just moved into the area!' Within minutes we were talking about old times and exchanging pictures of our children. Then she asked me what I was doing with myself that was interesting. Somehow I didn't want to tell her. I mean, who tells people that one's main outside activity is going to class to learn how to be a better mother? But when she mentioned that she was teaching handicapped children, I suddenly felt, why not? Everything we were learning here could be extremely useful to a teacher.

"So I began describing our course. I told her how we were learning to express our anger without doing damage, how we were helping our children to become more self-reliant, and about the wonderful things that had happened once we learned to accept our children's feelings. She listened with great interest until I mentioned the new way to praise. Then her old disapproving look came back.

" 'Describe what you see or feel?' she said, frowning. 'I don't buy that at all. Why go through such an elaborate procedure when you can let a kid know directly what you think? I don't see anything wrong in telling a youngster who shows you a well-made potholder that his work is good. Nor do I see any harm in telling him it's poor, if it is. I've never believed in coddling children.'

"I tried to explain that describing wasn't coddling; that describing was just taking out the value judgments.

"That really annoyed her. 'What's wrong with value judgments?' she asked, coldly. 'A teacher's job is to give realistic value judgments. How will a child ever make progress if he's not criticized?

" 'Besides, what's really important is that my students know that I'm honest. I don't have to resort to gimmicks. If they make a mistake, I point it out to them—on the spot. If they do something stupid, I don't mince words. I tell them, "That was a stupid thing to do." '

"I was shocked. 'You call the children "stupid" '?

" 'I don't call *them* stupid. I call what they *do* stupid. There's a big difference.'

" 'But Marcia, if anyone ever called what I did stupid, I couldn't help but *feel* stupid.'

" 'That's not the way it works. A child can make the distinction. Anyway, we're splitting hairs. It's been my experience that if the relationship is good, I can call a kid anything— "feather-brain," "noodle-head," even "stupid," and he'll take it from me because he knows I care about him and that I'm out for his good. And it might interest you to know that all my students are progressing beautifully.' "

Roslyn shrugged helplessly. "Well, Dr. Ginott, I had no answer for her. And the worst part is that now she's got *me* confused. She really does seem to care about the kids, and if she's that sure of herself and getting results, can she be completely wrong?"

There was audible indignation. Everybody had something to say. Dr. Ginott waited for the din to subside.

"Roslyn," he said, "here's how I see it. The most precious gift we can give a child is a positive and realistic self-image. Now how is this self-image formed? Not all at once, but slowly, experience by experience.

"It might help if we were to think of a child's self-image as wet cement. Imagine that each of our responses to him leaves a mark and shapes his character. This puts parents and teachers under a constant obligation. We had better make sure that any mark we leave is one we won't regret when the cement hardens.

"Let no adult underestimate the power of his words. Do you remember what your David once said to you, Jan? He said, 'My friends and me call each other stupid all the time, and it's just a joke. But when your mother or father calls you stupid— or your teacher—then you think it's true, because they ought to know.'

"Now what happens inside to a child who has accepted as truth that he's stupid? How does he meet the challenge of a new situation? Very simply. He says to himself, 'I'm stupid, so why try? If I don't try, I won't fail.' On the other hand, if over the years his strengths have been validated, he gives himself another kind of message. He says to himself, 'I'm capable, so I'll try. If it doesn't work out, I'll look for another way.'

"But Roslyn I can understand your frustration in trying to communicate these ideas. Descriptive praise is a difficult concept to explain. I've addressed parent groups, medical meetings, and teachers' associations; and while there is general agreement that constant negative criticism can be harmful, few people see any difference between a positive evaluation of a child's character, such as 'good boy,' and an appreciative description of his actions."

"You can send all the doubters over to my house," Katherine declared. "I'll be glad to explain the difference, because I've experienced both ways. For years my kids never heard anything from me but 'good boy,' or 'bad boy,' depending upon their behavior. It was the way my mother always talked to us. Then one day after a shopping trip with Chris, my five-year-old, I was about to say, 'You were a very good boy today.' But I thought, 'I'll try the new way. I'll really describe what I felt and what I saw.' So I said, 'Chris, I appreciated your help in the store today. The way you arranged the bottles and boxes in the cart in size order made shopping so much easier. Suddenly I had lots of extra room in my basket.'

"Do you know that since that day, he not only arranges the groceries in my shopping cart, but he's moved on to straightening his father's tool chest, my pantry, and now he's rearranging his toy shelves. He doesn't think of himself as a good boy or a bad boy anymore. He thinks of himself as a person who can put things in order if he wants to. Now, to me, that's a big difference."

"I have a story for the skeptics, too," Lee said. "I guess Michael was about eight at the time. The family was finishing supper and I was on a step stool reaching into the cabinet for a can of peaches for dessert. I grabbed hold of the can and suddenly I was doused with warm peach juice. I blew my top. 'Someone here is going to have his head handed to him!' I yelled.

"Right away Jason said, 'I didn't do it.' 'Me either,' Susie chimed in. But Michael never opened his mouth. We all looked at him. Then in a small voice, he said, 'I think I did it. I think I opened it yesterday and put the rest back. I only took one peach.'

"Well, just the sight of that worried little face and my anger evaporated. I almost jumped off the ladder to hug him and tell him what a wonderful, truthful boy he was. But my husband got to him first. He was fresh from the last meeting with Dr. Ginott's fathers' group, and he simply *described*.

"He said, 'Boy, Michael, I'll bet it wasn't easy to tell the truth just now—especially when Mom was yelling so loud.'

"Michael seemed grateful for his father's words and I thought that was the end of it. But the following week my husband and I came home from a movie and found a paper stuck to the kitchen door with a Band-Aid. It read: Broken glass. Do not walk in bare feet. From the person who did it. Your truthful son, Michael——And remember, his father never once called him truthful!"

Roslyn listened unhappily. "If I ever told that story to my ex-roommate, she'd scoff at it. She'd say, 'What would be so terrible about calling the boy truthful to begin with? Why beat around the bush?' "

"Let's consider that question," said Dr. Ginott. "Suppose Lee's husband had said to his son, 'Michael, you are a very truthful boy—the most truthful boy in the world.' What would go on in Michael's head? He'd think to himself, 'If my father only knew. If he only knew of all the times I didn't exactly tell the truth.'

"Suddenly Michael begins to feel anxious. He's being awarded an honor he doesn't deserve. He's being held up to a standard he can't hope to maintain. He's cornered. Trapped. How does he get out? Maybe he can misbehave a little—just enough to prove to his father that he's not such an angel after all.

"To a lay person it always comes as a surprise when he praises a child generously and the child then becomes obnoxious. To the psychologist it's no mystery. He knows that children must throw off global praise; it's too confining. As enlightened parents, we ought to be aware that when we use global praise with children, we are practically asking for trouble. I'm thinking of statements like: 'You're always so helpful. You're the most cheerful child I know. You're extremely intelligent.' "

"Ouch!" said Helen. "That sounds painfully familiar. Global praise used to be my specialty. I never passed up an opportunity to tell my kids *directly* how wonderful they were. I thought, 'The bigger the adjective, the better the compliment.'

"But my children didn't misbehave, they just didn't believe me. Billy would show me a drawing and I'd say, 'Fantastic!' He'd say, 'But do you *really* like it?' I'd say, 'Yes, I *really* like it. I love it.' He'd say, 'You're just trying to make me feel good.' Only when I described his work, in detail, did I see that contented 'Wow-Did-I-Do-All-That!' look.

"Roslyn, I suspect if your friend Marcia ever once saw that expression on a child's face, she'd find it hard to go back to the old way again."

Roslyn hesitated. "I don't know if I could explain all this to her. She'd demand a clear-cut example that related to her classroom."

"Well," said Helen, "Maybe I can be specific. You mentioned before that when a child brought her a potholder, she'd say, 'Good work.' Perhaps instead she could say something like:

'What a pleasure to look at these colors! The pink and orange are a treat to the eye.' Or . . .

'I like the way the stripes in your design go up and down. It reminds me of a Mondrian painting.' Or . . .

'Somebody's mother is going to enjoy a brand-new, original, handmade potholder!' Or . . .

'The quilting is so thick I'd feel protected from the hottest pot. *This* is what you'd really call a potholder!' "

"And that," Dr. Ginott smiled, "is what I call specific, descriptive praise. The point, Roslyn, isn't that telling a child he's 'good' is necessarily bad; it's just not good enough. It's limited. Helen's descriptive appreciation added a whole new dimension to the child's view of himself. Things have been pointed out to him that never would have occurred to him on his own. For instance, now he knows that he is capable of making something to protect another person. He finds out that his sense of color can give pleasure. He sees himself as being able to make something unique and useful. He discovers that his style is reminiscent of a famous artist. 'Who is Mondrian?' the child asks. Now the teacher has a motivated learner."

Roslyn answered, "I can just hear what my ex-roommate would say. 'Theoretically, it's valid. But what teacher is clever enough to be able to come up with that kind of response all the time?' "

"What we're talking about," said Dr. Ginott, "is not perfection, but a direction. I like to think of us aiming for seventy percent. But even ten percent would make an appreciable difference. When you're hungry, a little food is better than none."

I had been listening to the proceedings with mounting impatience. No one had mentioned the one thing that had upset me the most.

"Roslyn," I said, "I've been sitting here all this time, choking on the image of a handicapped child bringing his teacher a piece of work he's labored over, only to hear her call it 'poor.' And this she does proudly—in the name of honesty. I don't know anyone—child or adult—who ever improved from being told his work was poor. Besides, hasn't she noticed how quick children are to disparage their own work—to say, 'it stinks?' Would her answer to that be, 'You're right, let's be honest— it does stink!' "

Dr. Ginott seized upon this. "You raise a very important point," he said. "How *do* we help our children deal with their dissatisfactions? Suppose a youngster says, "My potholder stinks.' Our response might be, 'Oh, I can see you're not satisfied with the way your potholder turned out.'

" 'Yeah, the stitches are bad.'

" 'Oh, there's something about the stitches that doesn't please you?'

" 'Well, yes—they're crooked.'

" 'Then to satisfy you, the stitches would have to go in a straight line.'

" 'That's right.'

"This kind of conversation helps a child focus on what it is *he* wants to accomplish. Now he is free to go ahead and make changes. When we call his work poor, we stop him. We take away all his desire to go on."

Roslyn sighed wistfully. "I wish you had been with me the day I met Marcia, Dr. Ginott. *You* would have convinced her.

Not that she wouldn't have tussled with you. She has the kind of mind that looks for loopholes. I know her. She'd say something like, 'That's fine for the child who already senses that something is wrong. But what about the one who doesn't see his own mistakes? What about the child with an illegible handwriting who thinks it's great? Are you going to close your eyes and let that go on for years? You know it could hurt him in the long run!' I'd like to know how you would answer her."

Dr. Ginott turned to the group. "Would anyone care to take on the challenger?"

I volunteered. "I'm ripe for your question, Roslyn. About a week ago, David brought home his poetry report. Across the page on which his first original poem was written, the teacher had scrawled in red ink, 'Sloppy handwriting.'

"I couldn't get over it. Why would she deface a child's work like that? What could have prompted her to pick out one flaw and label his entire effort with it?

"For one wild moment I considered confronting her. I'd inform this person who was being paid to foster my son's intellectual growth that the way to help a child improve was to build upon his strengths, not to bludgeon him with his weaknesses. That if she wanted results, she would do well to begin by appreciating what he *had* accomplished, before ramming his 'deficiencies' down his throat!

"Oh well, a lot of good that would have done. . . . Anyway, when David handed me the paper I told him how mad it made me.

" 'It's true,' he muttered. 'I do have a sloppy handwriting.'

"He *believed* her! 'David,' I said, 'I think if someone's handwriting needs improvement, we ought to talk about how to improve it instead of calling it names!'

"Then I handed him a pencil and a fresh sheet of paper and asked him to write any three words he liked. He wrote his first, middle, and last name. It looked like my doctor's signature on a prescription—practically indecipherable. The teacher was right!

"I studied the paper until I found one respectable looking letter. Then I said, 'David, one way to have a neater handwriting is to get all the letters to stay on the same line. Take this *D* you made over here. That's a good example.'

"David bent over the paper and slowly formed the letters again. It was a little better. I said, 'You got the *v*, the *a*, and the *D* to stay on the line!' I thought we ought to quit while we were ahead, but David wanted to go on. 'What else?' he demanded.

" 'Another trick that helps, is to get all the letters to slant in the same direction, and that's not easy.'

"David said, 'I can do that, too.' And he did—more or less. It was far from perfect, but the improvement was so noticeable that David became very excited. 'Tell me something else to do!' he urged.

" 'The next step is the hardest of all. It's to keep about the same distance between each letter.'

"Again, David bent over his paper. This time he wrote very, very slowly. 'Is this right?' he asked.

"I examined it awhile before answering. Then I described. 'I see fairly even spaces between each letter. All the letters are on the same line, and most of them are slanting in the same direction. This penmanship is a pleasure to look at!'

" 'Actually,' David announced, 'I could have a very neat handwriting if I wanted to. Maybe I'll practice some more later.'

"I'm not sure if that example would sit well with your friend, Roslyn. She might feel I was overdoing it. But I don't know of any other way to work with a child except to begin with appreciation for where he is at the moment."

Roslyn said nothing. Halfway through my story I had lost her. I could see she was absorbed in her own thoughts. But Dr. Ginott was pleased with my example. "You gave David the freedom and the means to go ahead and improve his handwriting.

"A parent can be of great assistance to the child who's just been harmed by criticism. How? By translating for him, just as you did, Jan. We can translate the negative evaluation into a statement of what needs to be done. 'Sloppy handwriting' means *the letters need to be on the same line*. . . . 'Poor math skills' means *more drill is needed*. . . . 'Behaves rudely' means *needs to wait until others are finished before speaking* or *needs to express anger without calling names*. This kind of language can be of immediate help.

"But the best long-range protection against damaging criticism is a strong self-image. The child who thinks well of himself will recover much more quickly from an attack than the one who is already filled with doubt and self-hatred.

"It's recently occurred to me that a parent is in an even better position than a therapist when it comes to strengthening the self-image. Not only can a parent show appreciation for a youngster's present behavior, but he can also draw upon the past to bolster his child's self-esteem. It is mother or father who can tell Jimmy that he was an early talker, a collector of homeless cats, a daredevil of a climber. Who else would remember the way he got the kitchen clock to work again, the birthday party he planned by himself, or the time he cooked breakfast for the whole family because Mommy was sick. Each child has a multitude of small experiences that distinguish his life from any other. And each parent can be a living storehouse for his child's finest moments."

Lee nodded vigorously. "And it's a lucky child who has a parent with a well-stocked storehouse!" she declared. "A kid's past achievements can be a great comfort to him—especially when he's been called names by his best friend's mother."

Almost playfully Helen asked, "You have someone in mind?"

Lee smiled wryly. "Yeah, Michael. He came home so upset last Saturday he could hardly talk. From his garbled story, my husband, Hank, and I pieced together what must have happened.

"Michael and his friend, Paul, were playing tug-of-war with a stick. At one point, Paul must have fallen backwards and struck himself on the nose with the stick.

"Evidently Paul's mother heard his cries and came running. She took one look at his bloody nose and accused Michael of having hit him. When Michael denied it, she shrieked, 'You're a liar!'

"Apparently at that point Paul tried to come to his friend's defense. He told his mother that it *was* an accident—that they were both just pulling on a stick. 'Then you're both irresponsible!' she screamed.

"When the whole story was out, Hank sat Michael down on the sofa next to him. 'Michael,' he said, 'when someone calls you a name, what's important is not what they say to you, but what you say to yourself. Son, what *do* you say to yourself?'

"Michael shouted, 'I'm *not* a liar! I'm *not* irresponsible!'

" 'Well, it seems to me,' Hank said, 'that a boy who admits to opening a can of peaches when he knows that it could get him into trouble could hardly be called a liar.'

"Michael stared at him open-mouthed.

" 'And it seems to me,' Hank added, 'that a boy who sweeps the floor and makes up a sign to protect the members of his family from any possible broken glass—even though no one told him to do it—can hardly be called irresponsible!'

" 'That's right! I did do that, didn't I?' Michael said breathlessly. 'Tell her, Daddy. Go to her house or call her up and tell her about me.'

" 'You really want Paul's mother to know those things, don't you? . . . Michael, more important than anything I could tell her is that *you* know what kind of a person you are.'

"Michael left the room then. About twenty minutes later he was back with a funny look on his face. 'I just made up a proverb,' he said, 'and I don't know if you'll get it.'

" 'Try me,' Hank offered.

"Very seriously Michael recited, 'It's not what *they* think; it's what *I* know. . . . Does that make any sense?'

"I was staggered. In half an hour this child had gone from weeping to wisdom.

" 'Any sense?' Hank repeated. 'Why that's a profound philosophical observation!'

" 'Michael,' I said, 'I want that in writing, so I can look at it and think about it some more.' And do you know, I still have his proverb taped onto the refrigerator door."

Dr. Ginott had been listening with great interest. "It seems to me," he said, "that a child who can formulate that kind of statement has a decided advantage. He has a measure of protection from the mindless character assassination that children suffer every day. People will have a hard time locking him in with their labels—'Liar,' 'Irresponsible,' 'Lazy,' 'Feather-brain.' He has another image of himself to fall back upon. That image is his key to freedom.

"Lee, you and your husband have given Michael that key. Over and over again he's heard his special qualities and abilities described with appreciation. You're helping him to know, on a very deep level, what his strengths are; who he is.

"This kind of self-knowledge seldom comes to a person who

has been reared with constant evaluation. Life is more difficult for him. Often he remains dependent. He needs to look to other people to tell him who he is, what he can do, and how well he can do it."

Suddenly Roslyn came to life. 'Wait a minute!" she burst out. "That's it! That explains it all! I know just what I'll tell Marcia now. I'll say, 'You have no right to sit in judgment on other human beings. Your job is to help the children you're teaching believe in themselves, and they can't do that if they're always being evaluated. Do you want them to have to bring other people their potholders all their lives? The time comes when a child should look at his own potholder and say to himself, *'I'm* satisfied with what I made' or *'I'm* dissatisfied.' Sooner or later *he's* got to be able to decide what's right for him. 'What would have happened to Fulton, or Columbus, or the Wright Brothers if they had depended upon other people's opinions?' . . . What do you think, Dr. Ginott?"

"I think," he answered smiling, "you would agree with those psychologists who believe that in a healthy person the source, or locus, of evaluation lies within."

"I'm going to quote you on that!" Roslyn exulted. "I'll use it the next time I see Marcia! You have no idea how that will impress her."

Suddenly her hand flew to her mouth. "What am I saying! Listen to me. I'm still trying to convince her that I'm right. It's almost as if I've got to get her approval before I can have any confidence in myself.———Do you realize what I've been doing? I've been handing over *my* locus of evaluation to Marcia—depending upon *her* perception of what's good or bad, right or wrong. I've been letting her do to me what she does to her students!"

She turned to Lee. "What was Michael's proverb, again?"

"It's not what they think; it's what I know."

"Do me a favor, will you, Lee? Ask Michael to make another copy. Tell him you met a woman who wants to use it as a reminder. Tell him she plans to tape it on her refrigerator door, too."

Chapter VII
The Roles We Cast Them In

1. Mr. Sad Sack

When our group met again, it became clear that our session on praise had produced a windfall for the children. Our combined offspring had received more appreciation in the last two weeks than they had in the past two years.

"That's a hard-to-pronounce word you just used."

"I like your question; it makes me think."

"Almost an hour on the same puzzle? That takes perseverance! And concentration!"

Never before had so many egos been so well nourished. We felt like "very good" mothers.

If there were a single drawback, it was our overzealousness. Too much praise—even of the helpful variety—was sometimes experienced by the children as pressure. Helen reported that Laurie had said, "Motherrrr, you don't have to tell me it gives you pleasure *every* time I play the piano!"

A good point. We'd watch out for that. But the fact remained: Descriptive appreciation spoke directly to a child's heart. We listened raptly as one woman after the other gave testimony to the power of skillful praise.

Nell sat at the back of the room, apart from the group. At the end of one particularly glowing account, she shook her head.

Dr. Ginott saw her. "Nell," he said, "you're having your doubts."

Embarrassed at being noticed, Nell stammered, "No, not really . . . I . . . I guess I was just wondering what was wrong with me. Every one else has been so . . . Her voice trailed off. Then she blurted out, "Dr. Ginott, I haven't been able to find one thing about my son that's praiseworthy."

"And that troubles you," he said with concern.

"Well, it's an awful thing never to be able to say anything nice to your own child. If anyone can use a little praise, it's Kenneth. He's so lacking in confidence; he doesn't think he can do anything well. I guess he sees himself as a kind of nobody. You know, a mediocre student, a weak athlete. . ."

"How do you see him?" asked Dr. Ginott.

Nell thought for a moment. "Well, the truth is, he really *isn't* very capable. I know I should be more understanding, but sometimes I get so irritated with him. I watch him walking around the house with his shoulders drooping and that hangdog expression. It's as if he's deliberately trying to be a Mr. Sad Sack."

"You mean it's almost as if he's assumed a role for himself and everything he does must be in character?"

"That's right!" Nell exclaimed. "Even when something nice happens to him, he finds a way not to enjoy it."

She frowned deeply. "Maybe he *is* playing out a role. But if that's true, then what does it mean? Does it mean he's stuck with it? Is this the way he's going to be when he grows up?"

"It's possible," answered Dr. Ginott, "unless someone, at some time, sees him differently."

Nell looked bewildered. "I'm not sure I understand you."

"Nell, a child cannot disagree with his parents' true expectations. If our expectations are low, then we can be sure that our child's aspirations will follow suit. A parent who says, 'My child will never amount to much,' is likely to see his prophecy fulfilled."

"But Dr. Ginott," Nell cried out, "you said before that a self-image had to be realistic as well as positive. It would be unrealistic for me to have high expectations for Kenneth. The fact is, he *doesn't* do well in school. The fact is, he's *not* dependable. The fact is, he *is* careless."

"The question now," Dr. Ginott said, "is how can we help a child change from undependable to dependable, from a mediocre student to a capable student, from someone who won't amount to very much to someone who will count for something.

"The answer is at once both simple and complicated: *We treat a child as if he already is what we would like him to become.*"

Nell looked baffled. "I still don't understand," she said. "Do you mean I should try to visualize the kind of person Kenneth could be, and then act as if he already were that way?" She shrugged helplessly. "But I have no idea what he could be."

"Nell, here's how I see your son." Dr. Ginott spoke slowly. "I see Kenneth as a boy struggling to become a man."

Nell blinked for a moment, "Yes, but how could he ever . . ."

Dr. Ginott stopped her. "It's a difficult subject we've opened up. You may want to take some time to think about it."

Someone introduced another topic. After a brief discussion, Dr. Ginott consulted his appointment schedule. He told us that he was going on an extended lecture tour, and that it would be a month before we could meet again.

ONE MONTH LATER.

When the initial greetings were over, Dr. Ginott scanned our circle and fixed his eyes on Nell. "*You* have something to tell us," he said.

Nell smiled shyly. "Do you mean it shows?" She hesitated, as if in doubt over whether to go on. Then she spoke with great fervor. "You have no idea how the last session affected me. Dr. Ginott, I couldn't get your words out of my mind—that Kenneth was struggling to become a man. Every time I'd think about it, I'd start to cry. I don't know why . . . maybe it was just the picture of this sad, young boy working against all odds to achieve his manhood. And there was no one on his side . . . not even his mother."

Nell swallowed in an effort to compose herself. Then she continued. "Suddenly I had an overpowering desire to help him. He had such an enormous job ahead. I wanted to give him every bit of support possible.

"The next day I was suffused with my new mood. All my exchanges with Kenneth—even the most ordinary remarks—took on a different tone. For example, in the morning he came rushing back to the house for his sandwich; not an uncommon occurrence. 'I forgot my lunch,' he apologized. Well, instead of reprimanding him, I found myself cheerfully saying, 'It seems to me, Kenneth, you *remembered* your lunch—and just in time!'

"Then that same afternoon, after school, Kenneth asked for hot cocoa. Again I surprised myself. I suggested that he make it for himself this time, and that he make a cup for me, too.

"I think that really startled him. You see, I've never let him near the stove before because of his carelessness.

" 'How do you make it?' he asked.

" 'The directions are on the box,' " I said, and then I left.

"Three minutes later, the unmistakeable smell of scorched milk filled the house. I dashed into the kitchen and there stood Kenneth—his shirt, his pants, his shoes, all covered with boiled-over cocoa. He was a woeful sight.

" 'Boy, am I dumb!' he groaned. 'I can't do anything right.'

"Dr. Ginott, at that moment I thought of your classic illustration: 'The milk spilled. We need a sponge,' and I smiled inside. I said to Kenneth, 'Oh, I see the cocoa boiled over. You didn't want *that* to happen, did you?' Then I handed him an old towel and we both went to work on the cleanup.

"As Kenneth wiped up the mess, he mumbled, 'I don't know why I make so many mistakes.'

"I commiserated with him. 'A mistake can be discouraging. It can really knock the starch out of you. Do you know what your father used to say to me when I'd get mad at myself for making an error? He'd say, 'Look at it this way, Nell. A mistake can be a present. It can help you discover something you never knew before.'

"Kenneth turned that over in his mind awhile. Then he said half jokingly, 'Yeah, I discovered that when you're boiling milk, you'd better not have the flame too high.'

"I was so pleased to see his effort at humor, I tried to answer in kind. 'That's an astute observation, Dr. Pasteur.'

"Do you know, it was the nicest day we ever had together."

Dr. Ginott beamed. "The style is the substance; the mood is the message," he said. "What I'm hearing is a change in the entire quality of a relationship. Nell, I'm wondering if you're aware of how helpful you were to your son when he bemoaned all his mistakes. The more common response would have been to deny Kenneth's feelings: 'You don't really make so many mistakes. Actually, you're very smart. In fact, you're really a lot smarter than you think.' That kind of 'reassurance' would only have aroused his doubts and anxieties.

"I also noticed that Kenneth was a little reluctant to accept your new image of him. Often it's easier for a child to cling to his old self-defeating ways because at least they're familiar to him."

Nell listened carefully. "Then that might explain the business with the money!" she exclaimed. "Maybe he was trying to prove that my new confidence in him was unfounded. You see, the very next day, I gave him a five-dollar bill and asked him to pick up a few groceries for me, something I had never done. Well, he lost the money before he even got to the store.

"I was terribly upset. It seemed so deliberate, his losing it. I thought, 'I've been living in a dream world. He'll never change. He's just as irresponsible as ever.' I was too angry to even talk to him that night.

"But the next morning I awoke feeling calmer. Somehow I knew that I mustn't lose faith—that without my faith in him he'd be lost. So I did something that may seem very foolish to you. I handed Kenneth another five-dollar bill and the same grocery list.

"He was astonished. He said, 'You mean, you trust me? After what happened yesterday?'

"I said, 'That was yesterday. Today is today.'

"An hour later I was working at my desk in the bedroom when I heard a sound of something being pushed under the door. It was an envelope with change and a note."

Nell fumbled for a piece of paper in her pocketbook. She unfolded it and read tremulously:

Dear Mom and a half,
I got everything except the tomatoes. They were too soft,
Love,
Ken

"Did you hear what he called me? I'm not even sure I know what it means. And his signature! He's never referred to himself as 'Ken' before."

I marveled at Nell—this soft-voiced woman with her proper brown dress and her proper, almost out-of-date, manner. Where had she found the wisdom and the courage to do what she had done—and without a husband's support? I wondered what Dr. Ginott's response would be.

He said nothing, but kept his eyes on her—waiting.

"There's more," she said, tentatively, "but perhaps I've taken up too much time already."

"You have as much time as you need," Dr. Ginott said. "Please go on. We're all learning from a 'Mom-and-a-half.' "

Nell's face reddened. "But don't you see," she said, "none of this would have happened if I hadn't been coming here. It was a great gift to be able to feel more loving toward Kenneth. That in itself has made a tremendous difference; but it's the skills I've learned here that have enabled me to be helpful to him in ways I never dreamed possible. For example, at our last session, you spoke about a parent being 'a storehouse for his child's finest moments.' That would never have occurred to me on my own. Well, I started telling Kenneth about his early childhood, and he couldn't hear enough. One incident in particular from his nursery school days fascinated him."

"Tell it to us," said Dr. Ginott, "just the way you told it to Kenneth."

Nell paused for a moment. "I think I said something like, 'Kenneth I wonder if you remember your first interview at nursery school. The teacher was asking me a whole lot of questions about you. One of them was, 'Has Kenneth ever used scissors?'

"Before I could answer, you walked over to the play table,

picked up a pair of scissors and construction paper, and cut that paper neatly and precisely into two equal parts.

"The teacher was amazed. 'What hands!' she exclaimed. 'There's fine, small muscle coordination in those fingers.'

"Kenneth loved that story. But here's the point I'm trying to make. The very next day he bought himself a model airplane kit and worked on it for hours. When it was all finished he showed it to me.

" 'How did you ever get all those dozens of tiny pieces to dovetail into each other?' I asked.

" 'You know,' he said earnestly, holding up his hands, 'fine, small muscle coordination.' Now who would have thought that a little story from the past could mean so much to him?

"But that's not the end of it. About a week later my brother came to see us. His visits are very important to Kenneth; he's so fond of his uncle. We had a lovely family day. We went to church in the morning, took a long walk in the afternoon, and in the evening my brother stayed on for dinner. Kenneth had been saving an article from the science page of the school newspaper to show him, and asked if he could read it aloud at the table. He reads haltingly, but he was so excited by the content that he struggled with the technical words to get at the meaning.

"The article was about the first surgeon to transplant a human heart. When Kenneth finished reading, he sat up very straight in his chair, 'I know what I'm going to be when I grow up,' he said. 'A heart surgeon!'

"I was taken aback. Not only by his words, but by the way he looked—so intense, so serious. There was such a manly presence about him that I found myself staring.

"My brother broke the mood. He's a dear, but he's also a realist. He said, 'Kenny, forget it. In the first place, heart surgery is a limited field. In the second place, you don't have a prayer unless you have high grades, lots of money, and good connections. Besides, do you realize what a responsibility you'd be undertaking? Why, a person's life would be in your hands!' "Kenneth looked at me. His old beaten expression was back. "I moved in quickly, 'I can see what your uncle means. I suppose money and the right connections could present a problem. However, we'll deal with those difficulties when the time comes. But as far as having the responsibility of a person's life in his hands, well,' I gestured toward Kenneth's sturdy young fingers, *what better hands!'*

"In his whole life I never saw Kenneth look so proud."

A ripple of "ahhhs" filled the room. Someone started to talk, but Dr. Ginott made a staying gesture. He knew that Nell wasn't quite finished.

"I'm not pretending to myself that Kenneth is going to become a heart surgeon," she continued, "but I feel that his even thinking of it was important. I mean, no one with a poor self-image could consider such a thing, would they? And do you know, the queerest thing is *I'm* beginning to believe it's possible!

"Dr. Ginott, my question is, am I reading too much into all this? Am I overestimating the effect of my new attitude? Part of me feels I'm not—that I *am* responsible for the change. But the other part says, 'How could that be? The things I've said and done have only taken a minute here and there."

Dr. Ginott answered solemnly. "Nell, it only takes a minute to vaccinate a child against polio. But that minute protects him for the rest of his life."

It was what Nell had been waiting to hear. She sat back and took a deep breath.

No one cared to speak after that. Several women gazed off into space and a few walked over to Nell to share their admiration privately. I was gathering up my belongings when for some unaccountable reason I suddenly recalled my mother's unanswered question on the phone this morning.

"Janet dear, don't tell me you're still going to your course with that Doctor fellow! Don't you know it all by now? It's been two years already. How much more is there to learn?"

A lot more, Mama. A lot more.

2. The Princess

THREE WEEKS LATER.

The subject of roles was too intriguing to be dropped. We had many questions. Where does it begin—this business of a child playing out a part? At what point in his life does he become "the bully," "the complainer," "the dreamer," "the scholar," "the go-getter," "the problem child?"

Is he born that way? Does his place in the family (oldest, youngest, only child) determine his identity? What effect does his height or weight have upon his view of himself? His health? His intelligence? His physical attractiveness or lack of it? How about his peers? Don't *they* tell him who he is? And what about those events in his life that leave an indelible mark, like a death in the family?

Obviously there are many factors powerfully affecting a child that are beyond anyone's control.

But what are the ways in which a parent can shape a child's self-image for better or for worse? We wanted to talk about it again. To dig a little deeper this time.

One woman said that she had seen the most well-meaning parents do damage to a child's self-image in the spirit of fun. She said her own father used to tease her affectionately all the time. He'd call her Lazybones, or Miss Fumble-fingers, or Big Mouth. He was always "just kidding." But to her it was never funny. Even now, as an adult, she said, she can't quite shake off his words. There are still times she thinks of herself as lazy, clumsy, or loud.

Dr. Ginott nodded gravely. "You've learned firsthand that, even in fun, labeling can be disabling."

There was a thoughtful silence.

"Sometimes," said another woman, "a mother can do damage even when she's very serious about trying to help a child improve. She honestly believes that if she points out what's wrong, the child will then begin to change." She used herself as an example. She described how her son had lost his jacket; how she felt it was her duty to point out to him that he was becoming careless with his possessions; how she had listed other items he had lost that year—his key, a notebook, glass case, pen, and how at the end of her speech, he had looked at the floor and murmured, "I guess I'm just a loser."

She said that his response had startled her. Her intention had been to make him more responsible. Instead she had achieved exactly the opposite effect. From that day on, he couldn't seem to hold on to anything. He became "a loser."

Dr. Ginott agreed. "You've given an accurate description of how the diagnosis can become the disease."

Another woman had a thought. "I wonder whether parents don't sometimes unconsciously urge a child to play out a particular role, even though they might consciously deny it. I'm thinking especially of two friends of mine. One of them constantly complains that her son gets into so much mischief in school that he spends half his day in the principal's office. And yet she refers to him affectionately as, 'My son, the terror of P.S. 47.'

"My other friend always bemoans the fact that her daughter is overly conscientious, a perfectionist. Apparently this child gets into a nervous state unless everything she attempts turns out precisely right. But I notice that her mother will say proudly, right in front of her, 'Oh you know how Jennifer is —never satisfied. Everything she does has to be just so.' "

Dr. Ginott nodded again. "What you suspect may well be true. In both cases the children are probably hearing the parent's underlying message: 'Ignore my protests. Keep right on being a terror. Keep right on being a perfectionist. That's what Mother really wants.' When a child seems to be acting out a particular role, it's a good idea for a parent to ask himself 'What message am I really giving?' "

Lee harrumphed. "I suppose I should have asked myself that question about Susie seven years ago when she was born, though I doubt that it would have done any good. She seemed like a miracle to me—the first girl after two boys, and everything I never was: golden-haired, fair-skinned, delicate. I was awed by her.

"Now, with the benefit of hindsight, it's very clear to see what message she got from me both verbally and nonverbally, a hundred times a day: You're a precious jewel, an angel, a little princess.

"Well, I've learned the hard way where a princess belongs —in a fairy tale. Because in real life, she's hell to live with."

Dr. Ginott grinned. "When did you discover that the child was of royal lineage?"

"Three weeks ago," Lee said, "after listening to Nell tell about Kenneth. I went home and thought, 'Thank God I don't have her problem. Nobody's playing a role in my house.' Then Susie walked into the room and said, 'Brush my hair. And do it right this time!'

"I looked at her and thought, 'Does she always talk that way?'

"For the next few days I kept my eyes open and watched her in action. I saw how she operated. Whatever she wanted she got. First would come the command. If that didn't get results, she'd switch to her fail-safe method, temper and tears. This kid took from everyone—her brothers, her father, her grandparents, her friends—and gave nothing in return. Oh, if we were lucky, she'd flash us a smile now and then.

"All of a sudden it hit me. *My little princess is a spoiled brat.* The hardest thing to swallow was that my husband, Hank, had been telling me that for years, but I would never listen. What's more, whenever he tried to put his foot down with her, I'd interfere. No one should ever be mean to her!

"My guts began to churn. I went around the house muttering things to say to her, like: 'Kiddo, you may not know it, but your days of ruling the roost are over.' 'Doll Face, what you need are a couple of good whacks on the behind.'

"Then the guilt set in. What was I blaming Susie for? It wasn't her fault. *I* was the one who made her into a princess. *I* was the one who urged everyone to do her bidding."

Lee made a brushing aside gesture. "Well, that's ancient history. The problem now is: How do I undo it? How do I turn a brat into a person, a *mensch?*"

Her question hung in the air. We looked at each other vacantly. Most of us were still trying to absorb the fact that it was Lee who was having such difficulties—Lee, who had always been so strong and spirited and easygoing with her two boys. Yet here she was, the same mother, completely demoralized by one small girl. We wished we could come up with an instant solution for her.

But Lee wasn't waiting for any answers. "My first impulse," she went on, "was to get tough, come down hard on her, punish her, deprive her. Then I remembered, Dr. Ginott, how many times you said, 'To make a *mensch* you have to use *menschy* ways.'

"That really forced me to think. I thought about it all day—lying in the bathtub, standing in line at the supermarket, sitting in the dentist's chair. I even dreamed about it at night. Eventually, I worked out a two-part plan:

1. I would not allow myself to be manipulated any more.
2. I would look for ways to give Susie another message, another picture of herself. Not Susie, the princess; but Susie, fine human being.

"Well," said Lee heavily, "my new program has gone into action, and I hope I'm on the right track, because so far the only change has come from me. There's been precious little response from Susie."

"How would you say you've changed?" Dr. Ginott inquired.

Lee held up a sheaf of papers. "I'm afraid the answer to that could take up the rest of the session."

Dr. Ginott reassured her. "It will take as long as it takes."

Lee sat forward in her seat. "At the beginning I was like a cat, ready to pounce on the smallest sign of something that was generous or even slightly considerate. If Susie would just once do something that showed she was thinking of someone else, I'd make sure it didn't go unnoticed. But she gave me nothing to work with. So I made something up. . . . Does that sound crazy?

"One day after school, Susie was eating her way through the last box of cookies in the house. I thought to myself, 'Typical. It would never occur to her to leave anything for her brothers.' She bent down to scratch her leg and I snatched the box. I said, 'That was thoughtful of you, dear.'

"She looked confused.

"I went right on. 'Jason and Michael will really appreciate your leaving some cookies for them.' Her mouth opened, but she never said a word.

" 'Score one!' I thought. 'But how many times could I pull that off? There had to be a better way. Then it came to me. The way to teach *her* to be more generous was for *me* to be more generous. I mean, to do something for her that I don't ordinarily do. Kids never count the clean laundry, the meals, or the car pooling. They figure it's coming to them. So that night, while she was working on her arithmetic homework, I brought her a glass of cherry soda with an ice cube.

" 'Why'd you do that?' she asked, surprised.

" 'Thought maybe you could use a little pick-me-up,' I answered.

"Now there could be no connection at all, but the next afternoon Susie did something that gave me a little hope. I had fallen asleep on the sofa when I heard her yell to the boys, 'Shut up you two big mouths! Can't you see Mommy's sleeping?'

"It woke me; but hallelujah, she had finally given me something to work with! When Hank came home, I told him what happened—loud enough so Susie could overhear. I described how I had dozed off, how the boys had been very noisy, and how Susie had come to the rescue and quieted them down so that I could get some rest.

" 'That was very considerate of her,' Hank said, just as loud.

"For the rest of the evening she was livable with.

"Well, I've just described our more pleasant moments, when I was able to reach Susie a little. The rest was rough-going—all uphill.

"I soon discovered that when Susie doesn't get her way, she's got some mouth. I was called everything from 'Stupid' to 'Mean' to 'You're not a real mother.' And sometimes for good measure she'd throw in, 'I don't love you anymore.'

"I almost went under. Do you know what saved me? One little line in my notebook: *There are times for a parent to act, not react.* I hung onto that thought."

"What did it mean to you?" Dr. Ginott asked.

"To me it meant: Stop wasting your energy being hurt or trying to defend yourself. Start using your skills to help Susie change. . . . Well, that was no small job. For one thing, she needed to learn how to talk all over again. She was so used to demanding and getting, she didn't know any other way. It was up to me to show her that there were other possibilities.

"So I began. When she yelled from the bath, 'Ma! You forgot to get me my towel again!' I yelled back, 'Susie, this is the way I like to be asked, 'Mom, could you bring me my towel please?' . . . I'm still hoping one day she'll get the idea.

"Another time when I wouldn't let her watch TV before doing her homework, she called me mean and said she hated me.

"I answered her indignantly. 'That's not the way I like to be spoken to! If something makes you angry, then tell me: "Mom, that makes me angry! I wanted to do my homework *after* TV tonight." That way I'll know how you feel, and we'll see if something can be worked out.'

"The next time she called me mean, I was in a less generous mood. But I still didn't insult her. I had just spent two hours and seven dollars shopping for her required school supplies: For arithmetic, it had to be the three-ring hardcover; for spelling, the two-ring softcover; and the assignment pad had to be a spiral. After all this, that little stinker called me 'a mean witch,' because I wouldn't walk a block to the gum-ball machine.

" 'Young lady,' I said, 'Let me tell you something about your mother. When you call her mean, it makes her want to *be* mean!' I said it so fiercely, any normal kid would have backed down. But not Susie. She started to give me a fresh answer. I cut her right off. I said, 'What I expect to hear from you is, 'Thank you, Mother, for going to three different stores to get all my supplies. Thank you, Mother, for buying me an extra box of crayons. Thank you, Mother, for waiting patiently until I found just the pencil case I wanted.' ''

A few women applauded.

"Don't get carried away," Lee said derisively. "I sound real tough, don't I? As if I had all the answers. But believe me there were plenty of times I would have given up and given in if my husband hadn't worked along with me."

"May we have a specific example?" asked Dr. Ginott.

Lee thought a moment. "Last Saturday," she said, "Susie wanted a friend to sleep over. I told her I knew it meant a lot to her and that I wished I could say yes, but since company was coming that evening, I'd have to say no.

"I thought I had expressed myself rather nicely. Susie wasn't impressed. She launched into a full-scale attack. She stamped her foot and shouted, 'That's a stupid reason. All you ever think about is yourself and your dumb company!'

"I was so worn down I nearly took the path of least resistance. I was thinking, 'Do anything you want. Have a friend. Don't have a friend. Anything. Just leave me alone.' But fortunately, Hank was in the room and he held firm. He said, 'I heard your mother say that this is not a good night for a sleepover guest.'

"Susie didn't take kindly to that. She wasn't used to having her father cross her. She gave one ear-splitting shriek, ran up to her room, threw herself on the floor, and continued kicking and screaming.

"Suddenly I felt an overwhelming urge to yank her off the floor by her long, blonde curls and spank her—hard. I said to

Hank, 'I can't take that sound; I'm going to go up there and kill her!'

"He held me back.

" 'Then let her have her damned sleep-over friend,' I snarled, 'before she breaks the house down.'

" 'We're not going to let her intimidate us either,' Hank said calmly. Then he took a sheet of paper and printed:

Dear Susie,
   We can hear how upset you are.
   Screaming is not an acceptable way to voice your protest.
   As soon as you are able to talk or write, Mommy and I are interested in hearing from you.

Dad

"Jason delivered the letter, and we didn't hear a sound after that. He told us later that she came to him to ask what some of the words meant, and then she went to bed.

"I felt let down. I had hoped that with such a beautiful note my daughter might have come to us and talked things over. Maybe I was expecting too much. On the other hand, there was a positive side. I'm not sure I can even explain it, but all evening long with my company I felt good, almost proud. Hank and I had conducted ourselves like mature parents. We hadn't allowed a seven-year-old to bring us down to her level."

Dr. Ginott commented soberly. "To be able to deal with a difficult situation in a way that does not violate our values can be deeply satisfying. Lee, I'm seldom given to predictions, but I can tell you now, eventually you will see changes. No child can long resist this kind of approach. The combination of strength and humanity is potent."

"I hope you're right," Lee said. "Sometimes I get pretty

discouraged. Although something did happen yesterday that made me think maybe there *ha*s been a breakthrough."

Several voices asked, "What happened?"

"My father was visiting," Lee explained, "and brought Susie a present. She tore open the box and her face fell. 'It's the small Raggedy Ann,' she said accusingly. 'I wanted the big one!'

"My father turned white. 'Darling,' he said, 'do you think Grandpa didn't try? I ran everywhere. Finally I had to special-order it. I told the man I wanted the biggest Raggedy Ann they make for my grandchild. This was the size they sent.'

"Susie pushed the box aside. 'I don't want this. I want the big one.'

"Ordinarily I would have said, 'Dad, she doesn't understand. She's just a child. She'll get over it.' You see I was always there, right on the spot, to apologize for her bad manners. This time I stood up, took Susie by the hand, and said, 'Excuse us, Grandpa.'

"I led her into my bedroom and closed the door. Very slowly I said, 'Susie, when someone has taken the trouble to buy a gift, that gift should be accepted with a thank you.'

" 'But he got me the wrong size,' she wailed.

" 'I know,' I said, 'you were expecting one thing, and got another.'

"Susie nodded tearfully.

" 'In a case like that,' I said, 'it's a good idea to wait until the giver has gone home. Then you can tell your family or your friends how disappointed you are. . . . Do you know why?'

"Susie hesitated. 'So you won't hurt the person's feelings?'

" 'That puts it very clearly,' I said. Then I waited.

" 'Do you think Grandpa's feelings are hurt?' she asked.

" 'What do you think?' I answered.

"She shrugged. 'Well, I don't care!'

" 'I do. I think Grandpa needs to be made to feel better.'

" 'You do it.'

" 'All right, I will,' I said. 'But you think of something, too.'

"I went back to join my father and we didn't see Susie for a few minutes. When she came in, she was carrying a glass of cherry soda with an ice cube in it.

"She handed it to her grandfather. He gave it right back to her. 'No, darling, you drink it, he said.'

"I wanted to gag him. For the first time in her life my daughter was acting like a person, and my father was making a princess of her again.

"Nervously I waited to see what she'd do. For a moment she looked confused. Then she handed the glass back. She said, 'No, Grandpa, I made it for *you*. I thought you could use a little pick-me-up.' . . . Well, I almost burst inside. My feeling was: *She's going to make it. She'll be a mensch yet!*"

Listening to Lee at that moment, we too felt like bursting. Several of us started to congratulate her, but she stopped us.

"Look, I'm not kidding myself. I know it's only the beginning of a beginning. It took me seven years to make her a princess, and it could take another seven to undo it. But there's no going back for me."

A faraway look came into Lee's eyes. "You know, I had a small plant once on my windowsill. I never understood why it always seemed so lopsided. Finally it dawned on me. One side hadn't been getting any light. So I turned it around, and little by little, the whole plant began to straighten up.

"That's how I've been thinking about children lately—that they're like little plants. And if you keep turning them to the sun, they'll grow straight, too."

Dr. Ginott looked pensive. "And if it's not enough to turn the plant," he said, "we turn the sun."

3. The Whiner

WHY CAN'T I TURN THE SUN FOR HIM?

I walked out of that meeting aching with envy. Once in the street the women broke up into small groups—chatting, debating, laughing with each other. I lagged behind deliberately. I didn't want to talk to anyone.

I thought, "Why couldn't I help Andy like that? Why couldn't I free him from his crying, complaining, and endless self-pity? Why couldn't I turn the sun for him?"

I usually avoided thinking about Andy, except to tell myself he was going through a phase. Now I marshalled my full concentration. How does a spirited, outgoing child become withdrawn and miserable?

I examined every possibility. Could being sick so much that first year at school have been harder on him than I realized? All those sore throats, earaches, the steady round of antibiotics and temperature taking. Never being well long enough to make a friend. Could that have affected his disposition?

I wondered whether it was something I did or didn't do. Maybe I pampered him too much that year. But what could I do when he was lonely and wanted company or when he was cranky and needed comforting. Push him away?

His father may very well be contributing to the problem, too. He's been hypercritical lately. Not that I blame him. What man could listen to a steady stream of whining from his son, day after day, and not get disgusted? ("Who took my shoe? . . . I'm hungry. . . . It broke again. . . . I can't do it. . . . It's not my turn. . . . His is bigger. . . . You never take me.")

How I wished they had their old easygoing relationship back! A child can't grow with constant criticism. I thought of last night's episode. Andy had waited all day to show his father his latest invention and Ted had really tried to appreciate it. He got as far as an enthusiastic, "Hey, what have we here!" and then the familiar expression of disgust set in. "Look at you! You've got glue all over your new sweater, and I haven't even paid for it yet. Could you manage to invent something, just once, without making a mess of yourself?" Andy was devastated.

David is no help either. Although what can I expect from an eleven-year-old? Especially one who's had to watch his younger brother get the babying from Mommy that he's too big for now. I guess it's no mystery why he teases Andy every chance he gets.

All right, so it isn't anyone's fault. Just a combination of circumstances. But where does that leave us?

Helen's voice broke into my despairing thoughts. "Jan, you should see your expression! Is anything wrong?"

I tried to smile, but couldn't sustain it. Suddenly, my fears poured from me. "Helen, I'm worried about Andy. I don't think he's like other boys his age. He's so immature. I mean, by the time a child's eight, he should have some tolerance for frustration, shouldn't he? Andy goes to pieces over everything —big things, little things. It's not normal. A broken pencil, a scratch on his finger, the cat dying—it's all the same. Well, you know, you've seen him. He acts like a helpless, blubbering baby most of the time."

Helen stopped walking. "Hold it," she said slowly. "I think I understand what you're talking about. I know the part of Andy that's sensitive—that gets upset easily. But that's not the whole child. When I think of Andy, I picture a boy who's bold and imaginative. He doesn't just copy. He originates. He conceptualizes."

I didn't know what she was talking about. "You mean those little inventions of his?"

"Little!" Helen was indignant. "I suppose some of them are small in scale, but none of them is small in spirit. What comes naturally to Andy is what every artist reaches for all his working life—the courage to risk, to take chances on the unexplored."

"Helen, you're being kind, and I appreciate it, but. . . ."

"I'm not being kind," Helen retorted. "I'm talking about Andy objectively, albeit from an artist's point of view, and I tell you that to produce work of that caliber, takes great concentration, persistence, and maturity."

"Andy, mature?" That was an astounding thought.

Helen went on. "The whining and complaining is temporary. Maybe it's his way of letting you know that something is bothering him . . . but Jan, his *work* is who he is."

Right there on the street, I hugged her.

"What's that for?" she asked.

"You know."

One word more and I would have cried.

I spoke to Ted that night. I locked the bedroom door and told him everything—about Nell, Lee, the notion of roles and reversing roles—the whole concept of helping a child to change by changing the way you see him. Then I told him what Helen had said about Andy, and what her picture of him had meant to me.

Ted listened impassively. I became more intense. I wanted him to share my new clarity. I explained that maybe the way

I was perceiving Andy was his big problem, that until I stopped seeing him as immature and needing protection, he'd never be able to see himself any other way. Then I spoke of my determination to envision him differently.

What I had to say next was hard for me. I didn't know how to put it tactfully. I told Ted that I needed his help. I asked him not to be so harsh with Andy because it brought out the worst in me. One sharp word and I'd come rushing to defend my "poor baby" against his "ogre" father.

It was as if I had opened a festering wound. Ted spoke bitterly of his resentment toward me. He said he felt that I frequently cast him in the role of big brute, insensitive male, and that I was driving a wedge between him and his son.

I was stricken. I had no idea that Ted felt that way. I didn't even want to think about the implications. Quickly I swore that it wouldn't happen again, that I'd be different from now on. Then I pleaded with Ted that he be different, too. I reminded him of the incident of the glue on the sweater. I said, "Andy desperately wants your approval. He can't take your sarcasm. When he does something wrong, just give him a direction, like, 'When you work with glue, wear old clothes.' You'll see, he'll respond to that. . . . Well, you'd know what I mean if you were going to Dr. Ginott's fathers' group. Ted, do you think you'd ever be interested in joining?"

Ted suddenly looked grim. "No, I would *not* be interested," he said through his teeth. "I get the point, and I'll make an effort with Andy because I want to. But it's got to be my effort, my way. Don't put words in my mouth. If I say something that doesn't meet with your approval, I don't want to be corrected. And no evaluations either!"

A loud knock at the door. Jill's voice. "What are you two doing? You've been in there all night. I need Daddy to help me with my homework."

Ted went out.

Suddenly I felt bone-tired. When I woke, it was morning, I realized I must have fallen asleep with my clothes on.

Changes, many changes—some dramatic, some barely perceptible—came out of the turmoil of that day. During the next six months, I kept a log of the events and thoughts that seemed significant to me.

A New Role for Andy

THE NEXT DAY.

Can't wait to get hold of Andy, to introduce him to his heretofore unsung strengths—his imagination, his boldness, his perseverance, his maturity.

In he walks, pajama pants falling down, nose running, whimpering, "I'm not going to school today." I feel his forehead. It's cool. In the past, a runny nose would automatically guarantee him a day at home.

Not today. Today begins a new era. As of today, he stops thinking of himself as sickly. I say, "You have no temperature, honey. Do you want breakfast before you get dressed for school, or after?"

Andy looks at me in disbelief. Then he says, "I'll dress first."

My turn for disbelief. He really *is* going to school.

SAME DAY.

Andy returns home from school with a Little League application and a notice that tryouts will be held in a month. He looks into my face for my reaction.

I'm nonplussed. Little League has always been a dirty word to him. Could this morning have made the difference? Amazing! But he's never played any kind of ball before. And the competition's so rough, and I've heard some of the managers can be very nasty. He doesn't have to expose himself to that. . . . There I go again. I've got to cut that out or he'll read it in my eyes.

ANDY: Do you think I should join Little League?

ME: (*I translate fast. He means, "Do you think I'm capable?"*) So you're considering joining Little League this year?

ANDY: Yeah, but the managers yell at you if you miss the ball, and the kids make fun of you.

ME: I suppose that could be unpleasant. But you know what, Andy? I think you can take whatever they dish out.

ANDY: Yeah. Well, maybe I'll join next year. I'm not so good at catching.

So it was just a trial balloon. But he *is* considering it. Maybe with a little practice and encouragement he'd even join this year.

I nailed Ted as soon as he came in the door.

ME: (*Trying not to sound hysterical*) "Andy's been talking about Little League! You've got to take him out and teach him how to throw a ball. We've only got a month to get him into shape!"

SUNDAY.

Ted is taking Andy to the park for a workout. Both leave in high spirits. I hope it goes well.

Two hours later they walk in, silent. Andy goes straight up to his room and slams the door. Ted throws me a You-And-Your-Bright-Ideas look. He describes the whole disaster.

TED: All your son wanted to do was feed the ducks and collect rocks. I followed him around like an imbecile, trying to interest him in a catch. Five minutes before we left he did me a big favor. He let me throw the ball to him. Do you know, that kid's got fingers like spaghetti! . . . Listen, don't send me on any more missions.

Now they're mad at each other and mad at me. Ted is right. I shouldn't push him into activities with Andy. Whatever he does for his son ought to come from him.

I wish I could be more relaxed.

NEXT DAY.

Figured that Sunday for a minus. Not according to Andy. He keeps talking about the park. Asks where the ducks go when it rains, what they eat when people don't bring bread, and whether I ever noticed how the rocks change color when they're wet.

I'm moved by his wonderment. I say, "You have so many questions about the world. I'll bet men like Galileo and Da Vinci had your kind of scientific curiosity when they were young, too. . . . Andy, thoughts like yours deserve a notebook."

"What would I put in it?" he asks.

"Oh, maybe your questions. Maybe the things you wonder about. I have an idea that once you have the book in front of you, you'll know what to write."

TWO WEEKS LATER.

Andy's book is filled with observations—twelve pages of them. He's titled it, "My Private Book of Thoughts." The entry I like best is the one where he's drawn an outline of his own hand. Under it he's written, "A hand is like an island. Each finger is a peninsula."

ONE WEEK LATER.
Andy and I go shopping for a winter jacket today. Not much left in his size. In the third store he suddenly disintegrates. Cries and carries on so badly, people stop to stare. I empathize. No reaction. I ask for his cooperation. He cries louder. I give up. Let's go home.
On the way out, I stop off at the snack bar to fuel up for the long trip back. Andy gulps down his food and then before my eyes, I witness a total transformation: The squalling infant turns into an affable eight-year-old. "Let's try another department store," he says.

CONCLUSION: When a child is experiencing the physiological effects of hunger and fatigue, you may as well save your breath. One malted is worth a thousand words.

ONE MONTH LATER.
The whining is as bad as ever. Even when Andy's content, a whine seems to be his only way of expressing himself.
His family is no help, either. Jill and David love imitating him: "Wha—wha—wha." All he ever hears from Ted and me is, "Quit the blubbering." "You're complaining again." "Do you have to cry over every little thing?"
I'm afraid we're all just reinforcing what we want to get rid of. I think it's time to stop being so spontaneous. What Andy needs are some skilled responses.

THE NEXT DAY.
Preparing dinner feverishly, Andy wanders in. He bleats like a dying sheep, "I'm hunn-gary . . . I'm hunn-gary."

I say, "Andy, when you're too hungry to wait for dinner, tell me, 'Mom, I'm taking a piece of bread and butter,' or, 'Mom, I'm taking a carrot.' Or better still—just take it!" (A big improvement over "Are you complaining again!")

TWO DAYS LATER.

Today Andy comes to me with a long tale of woe. In an accusing voice he says that he hasn't had any loose-leaf paper for days and that I always say I'll get it for him but never do and that he needed paper at school and no one would lend it to him and that I had to take him to the store right now.

ME: Andy, I can hear you need paper and I plan to get it for you, but. . . .
ANDY: (*Belligerently*) But what?
ME: I didn't like the way I was asked. It made me feel as if a nail were scratching against a blackboard. I guess I prefer your other way of talking. You know, your deep, pleasant, manly voice.
ANDY: (*His voice an octave lower*) You mean, when I talk like this?
ME: That's it! You've got it!
ANDY: (*Looks at me carefully, then tugs at my blouse. He caricatures his usual whine*) Maaa, when are ya gonna get me paper. I wan paper.
ME: (*Holding my hands to my ears in mock horror*) Arrgh!
ANDY: (*Laughs. His voice drops still another octave*) Mother, I think today is a good day to go for paper.
ME: You convinced me.

When he was in bed that night, I heard him talking to himself. He was experimenting with both voices!

TWO DAYS LATER.

Same whine. Different script.

ANDY: You gotta take me for book covers. The teacher says we'll get a zero if our books aren't covered. I don't want a zero. You said you'd take me yesterday and you didn't.

He was so disgusting I had all I could do not to imitate him. I put up my hand.

ME: Andy, please. The other voice!

He ignored me and launched into a diatribe about how I had bought book covers for David and Jill but not for him.

ME: (*Firmly and slowly*) Andy, you have a hard-hearted mother.

ANDY: (*looks puzzled*)

ME: The problem now is to find the way to melt her hard heart. (*I left the room. Five minutes later Andy knocked at the bedroom door*)

ME: Come in.

ANDY: (*Straightforward and matter-of-factly*) Mom, I need book covers. Would you buy me some?

ME: (*Swelling with pleasure*) Young man, my heart is melted. Let's go.

In the car I thought triumphantly, "It's really beginning to make a dent."

NEXT DAY.

I've ruined everything. Returned from the battle of the January White Sales with six bath towels, four sheets, sore feet, and a headache.

ANDY: (*Plaintively*) Where were you? You said you'd be home at four. I'm hungry and there's nothing to eat. Did you buy me anything? What did you buy me?

Did I say, "Oh, you were wondering where I was? You were expecting me home at four"?

Did I say, "Sounds to me as if you were having a hard time finding something to eat"?

Did I say, "Oh, you were hoping I'd buy you something"? No.

I screamed, "Shut up! Shut up! Shut up! Your voice makes me crazy!"

Two steps forward, one step backward. I hope he's as strong as I keep telling myself he is.

ONE WEEK LATER.

That voice again! This time, it's something about needing money to send away for a special pump that you can only get from a store in Philadelphia. It's very sweet to see his young curiosity in ferment and I want to listen attentively, but that yammering sound makes me wild. I'm on the verge of another "Shut up!" There *has* to be an alternative.

I stop him mid-tirade.

ME: Andy, write it down for me. I can concentrate better if I see what you want in writing.

He doesn't like that.

ANDY: Write it! What do you think I have a mouth for? Just listen! I need an air-injection pump and. . . .
ME: In writing, please. When I see it in print I can think more clearly. I'd like to know exactly what it is you want, your reasons, and a rough estimate of the cost.

Andy stomps off to his room in a huff, but before he goes to bed, he hands me a sheet of paper. It reads:

Dear Mom,
I'm inventing a new rocket. The parts I need are an air-injection pump. It costs $1.25. I also need a fuel funnel. It costs 75 cents. And I'll pay you back.

Love,
Andy

That night while Andy was sleeping I left a note on his dresser.

Dear Builder of Rockets,
Your breakdown of expenses was so clear it helped me understand what you need.
Enclosed please find two dollars for supplies.
Happy blast-off!

Love,
Mom

TWO DAYS LATER.

It occurs to me that this business with Andy is absorbing all my energy. He's the first thing on my mind when I open my eyes and the last thing I think about before I go to bed.

No wonder Jill's been saying, "You never pay attention to me anymore." No wonder David is so actively obnoxious these days. No wonder Ted hides behind his newspaper every night. I've become a one dimensional character—Andy's Mother.

My life's been out of joint. I should be spending more time with Jill. And I should have gone with David to look at that new bicycle lock he's been wanting me to see.

But first and foremost, I've got to start paying some attention to Ted and me. Whoever it was that said children bring a couple closer together didn't know what he was talking about. It seems to me that mothering and fathering is a major deterrent to "manning and womaning." Well, tonight Ted and I will have dinner alone—chicken with wine and mushrooms. I haven't made it ín months because Andy hates it.

And I'm going to accept that invitation to Ted's alumni dance this year. I'll get his tux cleaned and buy myself a new evening gown. Why not? There's more to life than Andy!

ONE WEEK LATER.

Still in shock from what I heard this afternoon. Came into the kitchen to find Andy crying over a grilled cheese sandwich.

ANDY: (*Whimpering*) I burned it. I burned it.

ME: (*Shuddering*) Andy! That sound again! It grates on me. Just say, "Oh heck, my sandwich burned! I've got to make another one."

ANDY: (*Stares at the ruined sandwich, then speaks in a small voice*) But if I say it that way, you won't pity me.

"Oh my God!" I thought, "He's saying that he wants me to *pity* him!" I didn't know what to answer, so I said nothing. But all day long I couldn't get his words out of my head.

Is that how he sees himself—as a person who has no value for me unless he's the object of my pity? . . . What a terrible burden for a child to bear: to feel he has to make himself pitiful in order to be loved.

Maybe he feels that that's the way to make me happy—to satisfy my needs.

Are those my needs? I don't think so. Were they ever? Maybe—a little. . . . Well, never again, Andy. If that's what's been going on, then never, never again.

THREE DAYS LATER.

Something has changed inside of me. I hear it in my voice. It's lost its edge of desperation. I seem to have less need to be Wondrous Earth Mother, All-Powerful Giver of Immediate Comfort.

It's not that Andy doesn't try to stir up the old feelings. It's that I'm responding differently. I'm not even thinking about what to say anymore or how to say it. My words come from a deeper source. I know now that my son needs to feel his own strength, taste his own power—not mine. I look at Andy and expect that he *can*. I expect that he *will*.

A BOY NEEDS A FRIEND

A WEEK LATER.

Ran into Helen today. Found myself sharing everything that has been going on with Andy these last two months. What a pleasure to talk to her! For a while, I bask in her approval. Then she asks whether Andy has made any new friends this year. I explain that the boys on the block had excluded him long ago, and that the kids in his class were all, by his definition, a bunch of dumbheads.

"A boy needs a friend," Helen says.

I explain further—tell her how content he is at home with his collections and inventions.

Helen repeats, "He needs a friend. You can't be his friend."

I'm exasperated. "That, too? I've got to get him a friend, too?"

"No, but you can put him in a position where he can make one for himself."

"How?"

"Try asking his teacher's advice," Helen says. "That would be a likely first step."

Suddenly, I'm sorry I was so open. Helen's a wonderful person, but sometimes she can be overbearing.

SAME AFTERNOON.

All right. I'll see the teacher.

I guess he does need to get connected with other kids. I suppose there has been too much hanging around Mommy. Actually, there's no reason why he shouldn't be able to make friends. He just needs a little help to get started.

NEXT DAY.

Had a conference with Mrs. Miller, unbeknownst to Andy. She's a young, enthusiastic teacher, eager to help and full of ideas. She suggested:

1. Pairing him with another boy to work on a class poster.
2. Putting him in charge of the science corner.
3. Letting him choose "assistants" to clean the hamster cage and change the turtle's water.
4. Breaking up the class into small committees to work on projects outside the class.

Then she gave me the names and telephone numbers of a few boys who she thought might hit it off with Andy. She suggested that I lead them in some kind of group activity.

On the way home I thought, "Bowling! Of all sports, Andy is the least negative about bowling."

NEXT DAY.

Andy cool to the idea of group bowling. "Why can't we go alone," he says, "just you and me."

I mumble something about a club. The word "club" electrifies him. "We'll have a bowling club!" he shouts. "We'll meet every week."

A club it will be. I make the phone calls. All the kids are interested and everyone is free on Thursday. Andy prepares a shopping list. Tomorrow we'll buy soda and cookies for the first meeting of The Bowling Club. We're in business.

THURSDAY.

A fiasco.

The carefully-chosen cookies are thrown around the room, the soda is squirted at the ceiling, the boys are wild and very chummy—but only with each other. Andy is an outcast in his own home. Gets the lowest bowling score to boot. Doesn't want the club anymore. I push for one more try. No use.

Club disbands.

FRIDAY.

It's no good for Andy to be home every afternoon. Either he sits in front of the TV set like a zombie, follows me from room to room like a puppy, or he fights with David.

He needs to be away from home with other kids his own age! I'm beginning to sound like a broken record. "Andy, why don't you invite someone over today?" "Surely there's one person in your class you'd like to play with." "A boy needs friends in the afternoon."

Andy is resentful and resistant.

I become more subtle: "Some kid who likes to invent things is going to feel very lucky when he meets up with you."

Still no good. I know what's holding him back. It's my passion. He senses how much I want it for him, and that makes him want it less for himself.

How do I pry him out of the house?

THREE DAYS LATER.

I know what to do. *I'm* getting out. That new sewing machine has been sitting around for a year, and I still don't know how to thread the needle.

I track down an afternoon sewing class and tell Andy to make other arrangements for an hour on Tuesday since I won't be home.

Andy looks trapped. I busy myself putting away laundry and try not to catch his panic. He watches me for a while, as I methodically fold Ted's handerkerchiefs. Then he offers, "Well, my teacher says I have to stay after school to do a poster project with dumb Jim Plunkett. So I'll tell her I'll do it Tuesdays."

Bless, oh bless Mrs. Miller! She came through after all.

A WEEK LATER.

Craig calls. He's one of the boys from the defunct bowling club. Wants Andy to come to his house to play. Andy won't, so Craig comes here.

They're tentative with each other at first. Craig asks, "What do you want to do?" Andy answers, "I dunno, what do you want to do?" A little later I see them both outside poking around the garage. Finally they emerge with Ted's old rake and take turns gathering a huge pile of leaves. I watch them burrow under the heap like small chipmunks. For a while nothing moves. Suddenly a shower of red and gold autumn leaves fills the air and two boys emerge—shouting, laughing, tossing the leaves into the sky and onto each other.

Later in the house, over hot chocolate, they talk animatedly. Craig tells about his pet snakes and Andy tells about how his gerbil had babies.

That night, after Craig leaves, I see the old Andy again— gay, warm, outgoing. His mood lasts into the evening. He even volunteers to lend David his new pen.

NEXT DAY.

Craig calls again. This time Andy agrees to go over there. His first visit to a friend's house in over a year! It's been a week of firsts.

Andy comes home exuberant.

A MONTH LATER.

Friendship with Craig growing. Slow, but growing. Andy goes there again to play on Saturday. Craig has another friend visiting. Both boys gang up on Andy and throw sand at him. Andy comes running home distraught. There's sand in his hair, eyes, and mouth.

Between sobs, he gets the story out. Ted walks in, sees him whimpering, and says, "When are you going to learn to talk like a human being? Do you always have to sound like such a damn baby?"

Andy looks at me as if he has been struck. He buries his face in my stomach and I hear his muffled voice, "When I grow up I'm going to be a mother."

At that moment, if I had something in my hand, I would have hit Ted with it. Instead, I attend to Andy. I take him into the bathroom and clean him up.

Then I fly at Ted. I can't keep it inside anymore. I tell him what happened to Andy today and remind him how painstakingly I've been working to build this child's self-esteem. I shout, "Then you come charging in like a bull in a china shop and go smash, smash, smash! Don't you see what damage you're doing? Don't you care? He's your son, too, isn't he?"

Ted looks at me coldly. "I wonder," he answers. "Sometimes I'm not so sure." He turns his back on me and walks out.

ANDY AND HIS FATHER

THAT NIGHT

I lay awake with a dull ache in my head, going over the whole scene again and again. What a shocking thing for a boy to say, that he *wants to be a mother!* I'm sure he didn't mean it, but even so. And Ted's remark, about Andy not being his son. What was behind it? Does he feel that I take over with Andy too much, that I move in on his territory?

That's not true! I care very much about encouraging their relationship. I was the one who sent them to the park that day.

My words bounced back at me. *I* was the one who sent them to the park. It wasn't Ted's idea, was it? But I can't always depend on him to take the initiative. He comes home exhausted at the end of the day and has no resources left. When he finally does have something to do with Andy, it's usually to yell at him. It's better for everyone when I take over. . . . I guess I'm really saying that in a way I'm uneasy when Ted and Andy are together.

My head started to throb. As I lay there in that dark and silent room, it came to me slowly, painfully. I had done a grave injustice to both of them. I'd been giving Andy the message, in a hundred different ways, that he needs to be protected from his father!

Ironic. I've entrusted myself to Ted in the most important relationship of my life, and he's never let me down. Yet I haven't really trusted him with his own son.

Suddenly it didn't matter that Ted's temper was quick or that he didn't have my so-called touch. What Andy would get from his charming, vigorous, principled father would be the one thing I could never give him.

From his father, Andy would learn how to be a man.

THE NEXT MORNING. SUNDAY.

I say nothing to Ted about my new resolve. He knows me so well he'll see the difference.

After breakfast we linger quietly over a second cup of coffee while listening to music. Then Andy marches in banging on a tin can. Ted lashes out at him sharply. Andy turns to me with his He's-Being-Mean-to-Me-Again look. Normally that triggers my What-Did-the-Child-Do-That-Was-So-Terrible? look. But this time I simply said, "You heard your father, dear. We're trying to listen to music now. We need quiet."

Andy and Ted throw me a What's-This-All-About? look. I smile at both of them.

THAT AFTERNOON.

Ted explodes at Andy for borrowing his hammer without permission. Andy runs from him and wraps his arms around me. "Daddy's mean!" he cries.

Ordinarily this would elicit a moment of tender comforting from Mommy. Ted watches as I disengage myself and say, "I guess Daddy feels strongly about being asked permission before his things are used."

THAT NIGHT.

Andy comes to me worried about math homework. Says he can't understand fractions. I tell him to consult the math expert—his father.

They work together for ten minutes. Then Ted becomes impatient and Andy falls apart. "I'm slow," he wails. "I'm always the last one to get it."

"Andy," Ted says, "I don't want you to be concerned about fast or slow. It may take one person a half hour to learn fractions and it may take another person a whole week. But once they've learned it, they both know the same thing."

Andy pulls himself together and goes on.

I think: "And this is the man I was worried about?"

A MONTH LATER.

I've really stopped interfering with what goes on between Andy and Ted, and it may be pure coincidence, but I can't help noticing that Ted is taking over more and more. Occasionally he'll tuck Andy into bed at night and talk to him about rockets and motors. Last week they even went to the park for an hour to collect rocks. They're not completely easy with each other yet, but it's better. I feel as if a natural balance is being restored.

TWO WEEKS LATER.

It doesn't seem fair. Love *ought* to be enough. But I can see now that a parent can be a fine, decent, loving human being and still hurt his own child. I wish Ted knew some basic skills. He takes a minor issue and needlessly escalates it into a major confrontation. Last night, he started an all-out war.

At supper Andy reached for the bowl of mashed potatoes and scooped half of it onto his plate.

TED: Put that back.

ANDY: (*Clutching his plate*) No. Last time I only got a little bit.

TED: I said, put it back!

ANDY: You can't make me.

TED: (*Getting up and dragging Andy out of his seat*) Your dinner is over.

Andy called Ted a "big dope." Ted slapped him. Andy retaliated with a kick to the shins. Ted hit him again, harder this time, and pushed him into his room. Jill and David sat there taking in the whole scene.

When Ted returned to the table, we choked down the rest of our dinner. Finally the children finished their dessert and left. We were alone.

TED: I know just what you're thinking. The whole thing could have been avoided.

Fervently I wished it were tomorrow morning and that we would all have forgotten what happened. I could see nothing but an argument coming, and there had been enough bad feeling between us.

ME: Well, these things happen. He did take too much.

TED: I suppose I should have said, "Have as much as you want son. Don't worry about the rest of us."

ME: You know that wouldn't be helpful. He needed to be stopped.

TED: Right! That's exactly why I told him to put it back.

ME: (*Quietly*) You gave him a command. When you give a child a command, it makes him feel like defying you.

TED: Oh, I see. I'm not allowed to tell my own son what to do anymore. Okay, Teacher, what should I have done?

ME: (*Squirming*) I don't have all the answers.

TED: (*Sharply*) Don't play games with me. I asked what I should have done.

ME: (*Exasperated*) For one thing, you could have described the problem. For instance, "Andy, the mashed potatoes have to be divided among five people." That would have given Andy a chance to tell *himself* to put some back. . . . Or, you could have expressed your feelings. Maybe said, "I don't like seeing one person take half a bowl of potatoes. In this family we share." . . . Or, you could have given him a choice. You could have said something like, "Andy, that's too large a portion. You can put some back in the serving bowl or onto my plate, whichever you prefer." And there are probably a half-dozen other ways you could have avoided a contest of wills, only I can't think of them now.

TED: (*With heavy sarcasm*) That's what's so great about living with an expert. She's always there, on the spot, to rate you on your performance and tell you how you could have done better.

ME: (*Shouting*) You're forcing me into an impossible position! I don't want to be an expert! But I *do* go to a course, and I *have* learned a few skills and I can't rip them out of my brain or pretend I don't know them———I'm so frustrated! You make me feel as if I have a private corner on this information. I don't. It's available to you too!

Long, heavy silence. Dispiritedly I piled the dishes onto a tray and started for the sink. Ted mumbled something.

ME: What was that?

TED: I asked what night the fathers meet.

ME: (*Through the lump in my throat*) Thursday. . . . I didn't think you'd ever. . . . Thank you.

THURSDAY.

Ted has gone to the meeting tonight. I'm keeping my fingers crossed.

LATER.

He walks in, looking deliberately noncommittal.

ME: (*Unable to contain myself*) How did it go? What did you think? Did you introduce yourself as my husband?

TED: I certainly did. I told Dr. Ginott I've been looking forward to meeting the man who's bringing up my children.

ME: You didn't!

TED: I did, and he laughed. . . . You know, you never told me that his work went beyond children. Actually, he's teaching principles of communication that could apply to any relationship—business, friends, relatives, even nations. There's really only one exception.

ME: Who?

TED: (*With a gleam in his eye*) Wives who are already experts.

ME: (*Cuffing him*) You and your sarcastic tongue!

TED: Hey! Watch that. "Labeling is disabling."

ME: Hmmm. I don't know if I'm going to like having another expert in this house.

THE NEXT MORNING.

Ted comes in for breakfast and trips over Andy's sneakers

in the middle of the kitchen floor. I gird myself for the usual, "Andy do you have to be so sloppy? Put your sneakers in your room."

But it never comes. Instead I hear, "Andy, your sneakers are on the floor." Andy stares blankly at Ted. Ted repeats, "Your sneakers are on the floor." Andy answers, "Oh, okay, I'll put 'em away."

I don't know whether to be delighted or irritated. For two years now I've been after Ted to *describe* what bothers him instead of calling names, and he's ignored me. One evening with Dr. Ginott and he sounds as if he's been doing it all his life.

A MONTH LATER.

Aha! I knew it wasn't so easy. I see Ted start, stop, and start again. For instance, today he heard Andy accusing Jill of eating all the cherries. He started to say something like, "Cut it out. You're making a big deal over a couple of lousy cherries." But he stopped midway, and then switched gears.

TED: Andy, I can understand why you're disappointed. You went to the refrigerator expecting cherries and found a bunch of stems and pits. Now how can we make sure that everyone in this family gets a fair share from now on?

Another time Andy burst into tears because the store was out of the particular game he wanted and wouldn't be getting any more in stock until the following Wednesday. Ted said, "Now, Andy, don't carry on like a baby. You can't have everything you want the minute you want it. You've got to learn to be patient." Andy cried louder. Ted looked at me. I looked away.

TED: (*After a moment's thought*) It'll be hard for you to wait till next Wednesday. I bet you wish you had that game under your arm right now.

Andy stopped crying.

TWO WEEKS LATER.

I don't know what goes on in the fathers' group. Ted doesn't discuss it with me. But there must be some talk about the self-image because recently he's been saying things to make Andy feel good about himself. And at the most unlikely times! For instance, last night Andy was screaming over a broken record, hardly cause for praise. Yet I heard Ted say, "Andy, I can see you're upset about your record, but the kind of yell you let out just now should be saved for emergencies, like a fire. You've got a powerful set of lungs there, boy!"

And this morning Ted even found something positive to say when Andy knocked over his glass of juice. As Andy was wiping up the floor, Ted commented, "I appreciate the way you took care of that mess. No complaining, no blaming. You just quietly did what had to be done." Andy looked as if he'd been awarded a medal.

I'm tempted to tell Ted that each of his recent exchanges with his son could be used as a model for Dr. Ginott's principles. But I wouldn't dare. I don't think he'd welcome that kind of comment. So I'm keeping my mouth shut and enjoying the new atmosphere in the house.

THREE WEEKS LATER.

Tonight is bad. Ted very tired. In no mood to listen to Andy's mewling about how he still doesn't understand fractions. Ted lashes out with a series of biting sarcastic remarks. Then he glances at me defiantly, awaiting my You're-a-Beast look.

I don't give it to him.

Later he says, almost apologetically, "Gee, that voice of his grates on my nerves. I guess I was rough on him tonight."

ME: (*Casually*) So? So now he knows sometimes his father is rough on him. He's not a delicate flower.

FATHER AND SONS

THREE WEEKS LATER.

I have a horrifying thought. I'm beginning to suspect that some of the teasing and bad feeling between Andy and David has been due to me. It must be so because I notice now that Ted is breaking up the fights, the boys make up quickly and actually play together afterwards. I wonder why Ted's been able to put Dr. Ginott's theories about sibling rivalry into practice and I haven't. We've both learned the same skills. Why aren't they available to me when I need them? I guess sibling rivalry is not my forte. I get too upset seeing my own children attack each other.

Oh, if anyone wants to talk theory, I'm practically an expert. I know some teasing is normal and inevitable. I also know, hypothetically, just what to do about it.

I should protect the safety of the younger without making the older feel like a bully.

I should encourage the children to work out their own solutions.

I should diminish rage by allowing each child to express his hostility toward the other privately—in pictures, conversation, or writing.

I should make no odious comparisons.

And most important, I should never, under any circumstances whatsoever, take sides.

But when David starts picking on Andy, and Andy tries to defend himself, and David becomes harder and meaner, I'm suddenly five years old again, my big sister is punching me in the stomach, and I TAKE SIDES!

Not Ted. He's learned how to be on both their sides. He has a way of remaining neutral, and at the same time demanding personal responsibility from each child. It doesn't work all the time. Some of the fighting is beyond anything he can or even wants to cope with. But when he is able to use his new skills, I hear a sound that's totally different from my own.

For example, when the boys ran into the room like two raving maniacs each one trying to scream out his side of the story, I would have yelled, "I don't care what happened or who started it. I just want it ended!"

Ted, using Dr. Ginott's exact words, said, "You two guys are really furious with each other. I want to hear just what happened—in writing. Tell how it started, how it developed, what was said, and at the end make sure you include your recommendations for the future."

David would have none of it, but Andy wrote two pages. Ted read them aloud and discussed each recommendation seriously. Andy felt truly heard.

Another time Andy came in crying that David had punched him hard. David protested that it was only a play tap. I would have exploded at David, "How many times have I told you *never* to touch your brother? It can only lead to trouble!"

Ted said, "Andy, *you* felt a hard punch. David, *you* felt you were giving a little play tap. When someone feels something, then that's the way it is for him." Both boys stopped in their tracks and stared at each other. They had something to think about.

But when Andy really needs protection, his father gives it to him—again in a different way than I would. I'm thinking of the time David was sitting on Andy's back and pummeling him with clenched fists. My reaction would have been: "Get off him, you big bully!"

Ted pulled David off immediately and shouted, "When I see you hurting your brother, I feel like hurting you! You'd better disappear—fast!" David disappeared.

One more difference between us: I expect that because David is older and more mature, he'll be able to show more understanding and self-control with a younger child.

Not Ted. He never makes David feel he has to be nice to his kid brother no matter what. I heard him say to Andy (who was deliberately being irritating), "Son, you're playing with fire! David is trying to restrain himself, but don't take advantage of his good nature. Everyone has his limits."

But I think what I admire most is Ted's ability to help the boys when they're at an impasse. He's learned how to cut through the threats and name calling and still give full value to each boy's point of view by repeating it aloud. He's not always successful, but Monday night when they wouldn't go to bed because one wanted the light on and one wanted it off, Ted was most effective.

(I would have had an immediate solution for them: David could read in the living room until Andy fell asleep. And if they didn't like that idea, I'd think of something else.)

Ted got *them* to take responsibility for solving the problem.

TED: I hear a big disagreement.

ANDY: I'm not sleeping in this room anymore. He keeps the light on all night. I'm sleeping in the living room. He always gets his own way—just because he's older.

DAVID: That's not true, you little baby. You're the one who. . . .

TED: Wait a minute. No name-calling. Let's stick to the issues. Andy, as I understand it, you want the lights out at bedtime?

ANDY: Of course I do! I can't fall asleep when that "retard" has the light on.

TED: Andy, I repeat, no names! David, your brother says he has trouble falling asleep with the light on.

DAVID: How about me? I've got to read five books to get an A in English!

TED: I see. Andy, David's worried because he has the pressure of a lot of extra reading this year.

ANDY: Tough on him.

TED: It *is* tough on him, and it's been rough on you, too. When things are tough, we try to make them less tough for each other.

DAVID: How! I'm not going to fail English just because of him.

TED: It's a real dilemma—two boys who have different needs sharing the same room. . . . Look, I'll be in the living room reading. Take a half hour, kick the problem around, and see if you can come up with a solution that you can both live with.

Ten minutes later, with great excitement, they called Ted in. An agreement had been reached! David was going to give up the overhead light and use only his reading lamp. Andy was going to invent a light shield that could be attached to his headboard.

If this keeps up they may even get to be friends someday.

SATURDAY.

Ted is in a good mood—cheerful, despite a long list of errands. He pokes his head into Andy's room and invites him to come along. I'm pleased. He's never done that before. It was always David he took with him. Andy shrinks back. Even though it's been much better between them, he's still a little leery of Ted. Says he has to work on his rock collection.

Ted looks hurt, kisses me goodbye and starts out the door. Suddenly Andy appears with his shoes in his hands.

"I've changed my mind. I want to come."

"Good," Ted says.

They're gone for hours. It's dark when they finally walk in. Andy, almost euphoric, tells me about every detail of the day— the cool tools at the hardware store, the big saw at the lumberyard, the man at the paint store who gave him a free brush, the peppermint ice cream soda with chocolate syrup.

Ted gets me aside. He wants to tell me too. "We had some day," he says. "You know, I think the kid really likes me."

ME: What makes you think so?

TED: (*With a sheepish grin*) On the way home he put his head on my shoulder and said, "We had a real fatherly-sonly day today. Let's do it again soon, Dad."

A WEEK LATER.

I hope I'm not deluding myself, but it seems to me Andy has changed in the last six months. Not in any dramatic way. He still whines a great deal, but there are also times when he just "talks." He has a friend now, only one—Craig—but his first real friend. His brother and he still fight, but not as bitterly or as often. And most important, he's no longer tentative with his father. More and more he'll approach Ted first with a problem.

I know Andy has a long way to go, but I think a corner has been turned. He's not locked into his old helpless, whining baby role any longer. He's freer now to find his other selves.

THE EVENING OF TED'S ALUMNI DINNER DANCE.

Who is this elegantly-gowned, seductive woman in the mirror? Surely she's no one's mother!

Andy lunges for me. "You're pretty. I'm going to marry you."

"Stay away from me," I screech. "You've got tuna fish on your hands." There's not an ounce of maternal instinct in me. My entire concentration is on anchoring my Grecian wiglet. Tonight is for grown-ups.

It was a beautiful party. Sumptuous food, lovely music, charming people—so civilized. Not one person had a temper tantrum and everyone cut his own meat.

We were all reluctant to end the evening. Ted's old friend invited a few couples back to his apartment. Over coffee, the conversation rambled pleasantly—vacations, whatever-became-of, city versus suburbia, and children.

Children! Who wanted to talk about children in evening clothes? I tried not to listen—to hold onto the festive mood. But the comments penetrated my glow.

"There's no doubt about it, kids come into this world with different personalities. Take my youngest; sweet, good-natured, he'd give you the shirt off his back. But the oldest won't part with a dime. He's a born miser."

"I know what you mean. I've got one at Princeton, and another who'll be lucky if he gets out of high school. He'll never be a student—that's for sure. I've told him, 'You're not stupid, just lazy.' "

"You should meet my daughters. You wouldn't know they were related. The little one is graceful—moves like a ballerina —and the big one can't walk into a room without knocking something over. We call her 'The Klutz.' "

Someone laughed.

"How about your kids, Ted? You've got three, haven't you? What are they like?"

I tensed. Ted shrugged. "They're like———whatever they can be. Different people at different times."

"Never mind the philosophy. That's no answer. C'mon, you tell us, Jan."

It flashed through my mind that there was a time when I could have joined them comfortably in their round of type-casting. But now there was a chasm of experience between us. They hadn't heard about Kenneth or Susie. They didn't know about Andy. Should I tell them? No. Much too personal. Besides, it was hardly party talk.

Everyone looked at me expectantly. I smiled lamely and mumbled that they were all invited to the house to meet the children and see for themselves.

Someone noticed the lateness of the hour. There was a sudden gathering of coats, a babble of goodbyes, and promises to see each other more often. Downstairs, I sat in the lobby and waited for Ted to get the car. The last part of the conversation left an unpleasant aftertaste. It bothered me that I hadn't been honest. I wouldn't have had to bare my soul with a personal case history, but I could have said something. What?

If I were really free to express myself, I could have told them: Dear friends, what you're making jokes about is no laughing matter. Children see themselves primarily through their parents' eyes. They look to us to tell them not necessarily what they are, but what they're capable of becoming. They depend upon us for a larger vision of themselves, and for the tools to implement that vision.

I could have told them:

There is no such thing as a child who is "selfish." There's only a child who needs to experience the joys of generosity.

There is no such thing as a child who is "lazy." There's only a child who is unmotivated, who needs someone to believe that he can work hard when he cares enough.

There is no such thing as a child who is "clumsy." There's only a child who needs to have his movements accepted and his body exercised.

Children—all children—need to have their best affirmed and their worst ignored or redirected.

And who will undertake this challenging job?

Parents.

Who but a parent would be willing to make changes within himself so that in time his child might change?

Who but a parent has the largeness of spirit to tell the erring child, "That was then. This is now. Let's begin again."

Who but a parent cares enough to say to the dirty ragamuffin, "Come, I believe in you. I see *beneath* your tattered layers. I shall clothe you in the radiant garments of a prince, and you shall indeed become one."

THE NEXT DAY.

Just reread what I wrote last night. It's a good thing I held my tongue. I couldn't have said anything like that to those people. Much too preachy.

But it's strange, somehow in "telling them" I told myself.

I think I know it now.

This will be the last entry in my diary.

Chapter VIII

Don't Change a Mind :
Change a Mood

When David was an infant, I'd sit in the playground, jiggle his carriage, and listen to the women around me commiserate with each other on how hard it was to get their children to "mind."

Brian didn't brush his teeth even though his mother kept warning him he'd get cavities. Julie wouldn't pick up her toys despite daily lectures on neatness. And Lewis had to be reminded to flush the toilet every time he used it.

I'd think to myself, "Gee, they're a cheerless bunch. I feel sorry for their kids."

Now, three children later, I'm less critical. I've discovered that the constant effort to get a child to do what I consider vital and he considers superfluous can knock the cheer out of you. I don't think I'm alone, either. I suspect that most parents become distressed by disorder, grim about green teeth, and revolted by reeking toilet bowls. Therefore, whenever a mother in our group reports how she engaged her child's cooperation

126

pleasantly, without moralizing, lecturing, or warning of dire consequences, I'm always impressed.

I'm thinking particularly of Katherine. She has a way of setting the kind of mood that reduces resistance. Even when she has to prod or remind, she'll do it with a very light touch: "Chris, I didn't hear the toilet flush." Or, "Patty, toothbrushing before bedtime!" Or, "Children, I need help with the dishes." (All simple descriptive statements.)

Usually she consults their preference about how and when chores are to be done: "Would you like to do the dishes before dessert or after?" "Would you rather use a dish cloth or a scouring pad?" But her manner communicates that when she asks for help, she expects to get it.

I also like her approach when a job doesn't meet her standards. She never attacks a child's efforts ("Can't you do anything right?") but rather gives full appreciation to what *has* been accomplished before pointing out what else needs to be done. She'll say, "Well, Chris, it must have taken a lot of elbow grease to get the pan this clean. There are just a few stubborn bits of dried egg left on the side here."

Katherine claims that even though she avoids the usual bossing and blaming, only one thing really saves her from becoming a classic nag, and that's routine. Flexible routine. She keeps a bulletin board in the kitchen where the children are constantly tacking up and changing schedules that they've worked out themselves. Instead of getting into long arguments over who walks the dog or sorts the laundry, Katherine will say, "Check today's schedule." Consequently, most of the grumbling is done at the chart on the wall, instead of at mother.

Recently, the children devised something new—a workwheel for kitchen chores. Each week the wheel turns to assign another set of duties.

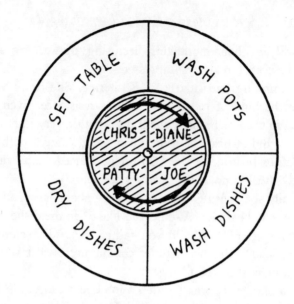

Obviously Katherine's pleasant, no-nonsense manner creates the kind of family spirit that makes everyone feel good about working together.

There is yet another approach that invites cooperation. Although I hesitate to mention it here. For who will believe that in a situation that normally triggers a battle, some parents actually manage to be funny. Playfulness instead of polemics? Humor instead of a hassle? To me this seems above and beyond.

Helen feels differently. She says for her, play is practically a necessity—a way of toning down her intensity and neutralizing her natural bossiness. When she can kid around about a job that has to be done, there's a double benefit. She becomes more relaxed, and the children less resistant. They enjoy it most when she slips into another character.

For example: One afternoon Laurie and Billy were about to go off to the store in a downpour, wearing only sandals and light tee shirts. With dread, Helen foresaw the whole argument.

"Children, it's raining."

"No, it's only drizzling."

"I'd like you to wear your rain gear."

"But we're only going out for a little while."

"You'll get soaked."

"We'll run."

In a moment of manic inspiration she assumed a Donald Ducklike voice. "What, no waincoat or wubbers?" she quacked. "I'm vewy supwised. I thought all widdle ducks wuv to wear waincoats and wubbers when it wains."

The children broke into giggles, and headed for the closet, talking "duck talk" on the way.

Another time, Billy and Laurie were leaving the house before their rooms were cleaned. Helen collared them at the door. In her toughest gangster voice she rasped, "Okay, you guys, freeze! I just cased the back rooms and they're a mess. Nobody leaves town until this joint gets straightened out. See? And it better be a clean job or the big boss ain't gonna like it. Got that?"

One more zany example. Helen was watching a TV program with Billy about farm life. At one point she had the distinct impression she could actually smell the animals on the screen. In confusion she sniffed the air. Next to her on the sofa Billy shifted his position. Suddenly she knew from whence the fumes were emanating.

After the program Helen twanged, "William, smells like you bin out huntin' skunk! Now git yer hide into the old tin tub and give yourself a good scrubbin' with brown soap and a stiff brush. I want you smellin' decent agin 'fore Paw gets home. . . . And no back talk 'bout how you jest had a bath last year. Yer gittin old enough to bathe twicet a year now!"

Lee said she'd like to be more jovial with all of her children, but it's not that easy. Jason takes life very seriously. Any attempt at humor with him is usually met with, "Ha, ha, very funny." Susie, on the other hand, will just stare at her blankly —hardly an inspiration to go on. It's Michael who brings out her sense of fun.

Even when he's half asleep he's ready for play. Lee told us how one morning she went to wake him and found an amorphous shape on the bed completely covered. "Hey," she said, "I see a submarine under there. Would it like to surface? Poke its periscope out of the blanket? Or does it want to lie submerged for another five minutes?" Michael stuck out one finger and wiggled it.

Another time she found him sitting on his bed, obviously overwhelmed by the cleanup that lay ahead. "No wonder," thought Lee, looking at the layers of debris on his floor, "he has no place to put anything."

She went downstairs and was back a few minutes later with an armful of empty shoe boxes and a record.

"Michael," she said, "just because putting a room in order is hard work doesn't mean we have to let it get us down. Today we're going to lick the cleanup blahs."

She put a march on the record player. "We'll have music to rouse our spirits," she shouted over the Marine Corps Band, "and here are lots of boxes, so you'll have room to store all your special treasures."

Michael broke into a grin and slid off the bed onto the floor. Then, in time to the music, he began tossing marbles in one box and checkers into another.

Roslyn says she can handle a problem situation playfully, but only later, never on the spot. Not until the children are out of sight, sleeping soundly, and the whole house quiet, does her sense of humor return. Somehow as soon as she puts pen to paper, she starts to feel better. Her first drafts are almost always mean, sarcastic, and highly satisfying. Then, little by little she edits, rephrases, until she makes her point without accusation. Here are some deadlocked situations that yielded to her notes.

When the children came to a standstill over brushing teeth, she drew a sign and pasted it on the bathroom mirror.

WHICH TEETH ARE YOURS?

When bedtime became an exhausting nightly battle, Roslyn composed a letter, typed it, and placed a copy on each child's pillow. It read.

Thoughts About Bedtime

WHEREAS: Early to bed
With a smile and good cheer
Make parents a pleasure,
A joy to be near!

WHEREAS: The opposite is also true; namely:
Late to bed with reminders and warnings
Make parents cantankerous
And mornings for mourning.

> *We hereby invite your suggestions for a bedtime hour that will restore this family's peace and harmony. Please fill in the blanks below.*
>
> *I think I should be in bed between ____ and ____.*
> *I think "lights out" should be between ____ and ____.*
>
> Love,
> Mom

When Roslyn found herself nagging for help in the kitchen, and getting nowhere, she made up the following notice and posted it on the pantry door.

BULLETIN

CRISIS IN THE KITCHEN

When last seen, the cook of the Davis Diner was reported to be stomping around the kitchen, threatening to resign.

A trusted inside source saw her angrily beating up the mashed potatoes and muttering, "It's too much for one person! I can't run a whole restaurant by myself!"

Because of this dire emergency, we urge all steady customers to volunteer their services immediately.

Workers are needed to

> ____*Clear tables*
> ____*Rinse china and flatware*
> ____*Load dishwasher*
> ____*Shine pots and pans*
> ____*Sweep floor*

Please check and initial any two jobs you prefer.
P.S. No experience necessary.
Free on-job training.

So apparently some parents do exist who can avoid the usual locking of horns and establish through humor, a spirit of friendly cooperation. No mean accomplishment!

But there's more to be said for the value of a good mood. Its benefits extend far beyond the purely practical ones of gaining cooperation. When a good mood prevails, good things often happen. Old and young alike tend to become more expansive, more responsive, even more inventive. The improbable suddenly becomes possible. Loving impulses are released which happily infect the entire household.

A bad mood can be just as contagious! Not until I had a family of my own could I fully appreciate how easy it is to catch children's negative feelings. My own tendency is to become irritable when a child is irritable, discouraged when he's discouraged, and ultimately to join him in making matters worse. Therefore, whenever someone in our group reports how she actually managed to separate herself from her child's mood, and reverse the downward spiral, I'm confounded.

Listening to these accounts brings back the same sense of wonder I had as a child watching the cartoon rabbit plummet over the edge of a cliff. Who could predict that at the last unbearable moment, his ears would turn into wings, his tail into a propeller, and he would zoom upward, defying gravity.

Here are two of my favorite They'll-Never-Get-Out-of-This-One stories. In each of them a parent succeeds in changing the mood against the odds.

The first I call:

ERASE

(In this story Helen saves the day by using Dr. Ginott's formula for a dead-end situation: "Erase and begin again.")

SCENE: *Early morning, Laurie's bedroom.*
LAURIE: Mommy, what should I wear today?
HELEN: How about one of those adorable new skirts we bought for school? They've just been hanging in the closet.

LAURIE: I don't like them.

HELEN: Honey, *you* were the one who picked them out! Here, you can wear this plaid kilt. You'll look like a Scottish lassie in it.

LAURIE: I don't want to look like a Scottish lassie. I want to wear pants.

HELEN: But you always wear pants. It's time for a change. If you don't want the kilt, then how about the blue skirt with brass buttons?

LAURIE: That one itches.

HELEN: Then you could wear a little slip under it.

LAURIE: (*On the verge of tears*) I hate slips!

HELEN: (*To herself*) I'm doing it again. Imposing my taste. Not letting her make a simple decision for herself . . . How do I untangle this one? (*Aloud*) Laurie, let's "erase."

LAURIE: Huh?

HELEN: Let's erase and start all over again. Let's pretend I've just come up the stairs to wake you.

Helen: (*Walks out, closes the door behind her, waits a moment, then knocks.*)

LAURIE: (*Reluctantly going along*) Come in.

HELEN: Good morning. Did I hear someone ask me what to wear today?

LAURIE: Uh huh.

HELEN: Well, before a person knows what to wear, she may have to ask herself how she feels. "Am I in an old brown pants mood today or in a new skirt mood? Do I feel like a fuzzy yellow sweater or do I feel like my flowered print blouse?"

LAURIE: (*Taking her time to think*) I feel like . . . my blue sweater and my old brown pants.

HELEN: Here's an eight-year-old who really knows her own mind!

LAURIE: (*Confiding shyly*) Blue is my favorite color.

MICHAEL AND THE KANGAROO

(In this story Lee changes the atmosphere with a touch of fantasy.)

One afternoon Lee caught Michael growling ferociously at Muffin, the new puppy. She asked him to stop. He insisted that Muffin knew he was only playing and then began to butt the dog with his head.

Lee thought, "How can I get through to him? Forbid him to go near the puppy for a week? Threaten to tell his father? Lecture him sternly?" She was already formulating a speech on cruelty to animals when she suddenly recalled Dr. Ginott saying, "*Don't change a mind; change a mood.*" She wondered whether she could.

LEE: Michael, I can see how much you like to roughhouse . . . You know what we should have done? Sent away to Australia, and mail-ordered you a kangaroo—complete with boxing gloves.

Michael stopped growling and looked up. The puppy retreated to a corner.

LEE: (*Warming to her subject*) We could have built him a little cot with a special hole for his tail.
MICHAEL: (*Giggling*) He could have slept in my room.
LEE: Right next to your bed! You would have had a sparring partner ready and waiting anytime you wanted to throw a few punches.

Lee knelt down on the floor and spoke softly to the dog.

LEE: You're no kangaroo, are you Muffin? You're just a little pup and you don't care for rough play at all.

Michael crouched down beside her and smoothed Muffin's fur.

LEE: (*Continuing to talk to the dog*) You like to be stroked, and patted, and played with gently, don't you, pooch?

MICHAEL: (*Rubbing his nose cautiously against the puppy's nose*) Very, very gently.

I don't know what it is about these stories that moves me so. I suppose it's the notion of parents being able to transcend the grim moment, gracing it with humor and imagination. What a nice way to live! But I'm enough of a realist to know that humor is a sometime thing—not a matter of will or skill, either there at the moment or not, nothing that can be summoned up on demand.

So far I've credited only adults with the ability to originate a good mood. But I'd be remiss if I closed this chapter without mentioning the true prodigies of playfulness, the master acrobats of the quick mood change—the children themselves. They're the ones who can bounce from moping to merriment with an agility long lost to grown-ups. And often they come up with the kind of contribution that no adult would ever dream of. Luckily, they lack our inhibitions.

I offer one small example from my own family.

We were all in the car one evening returning home from a Little League game. We rode in total silence. Four times David had come up to bat—and four times the whole family had watched as he struck out. His gloom filled every corner of the car. I'd have given anything to be able to change the mood then. I thought hard. Nothing came. Finally David spoke.

DAVID: I don't belong in Little League. I don't even belong in the Farm League. I belong in the Diaper League.

FATHER: Gee, David, I have to admire that. You're feeling so low, but you still haven't lost your sense of humor. . . . I wonder how they'd keep score in the Diaper League.

DAVID: (*Morosely*) I guess if you made "number one" you'd get on first base.

JILL: (*Becoming interested*) Then to get on second, you'd have to make "number two."

From the back seat of the station wagon Andy bounced up and down in a fever of excitement.

ANDY: I know what a home run would be!

We all turned to him.

ANDY: (*Triumphantly*) Diarrhea!

Five people burst out laughing.

See what I mean?

PARENTS ARE PEOPLE

Chapter IX

We Feel What We Feel

I had been leafing through my notebook. Each time I read one of Dr. Ginott's statements regarding parents' feelings, I bristled.

"A parent should respect his own limits."

"We can be a little nicer than we feel, but not much."

"It is important to accept the reality of our feelings of the moment."

"It's best to be authentic with our children."

Why did I react so strongly to these statements? They seemed perfectly reasonable—perfectly logical. I studied them again. And then it occurred to me. Underlying each of these statements was the assumption that a person usually knows what he feels. The more I dwelt upon it, the more uncomfortable I became. *Maybe I didn't always know what I felt!*

The thought unsettled me. I tried to reassure myself. "Nonsense! You know precisely how you feel about a whole range of controversial subjects—women's liberation, legalizing marijuana, welfare legislation, Middle-East tensions, busing, co-ed dormitories. Nothing wishy-washy about you. You're clarity personified!"

But I wasn't convinced. Deep down I knew where my confusion lay. It was with the children. Let just one child descend upon me, and all clarity vanished. That internal mechanism—the one I counted on to send me clear signals about my feelings—seemed to go haywire whenever the children came upon the scene.

It was almost funny, and the joke seemed to be on me. The mother who was so dedicated to helping her children get in touch with *their* feelings was probably out of touch with her own.

Take last Sunday for example. I was curled up with the paper when the children burst in with "Mommy, Daddy promised we could go for ice cream. Now he says it will take him all afternoon to finish paying bills!" I thought, "Oh they were looking forward to it. *I'll* take them." Pushing the papers aside, I dug myself out of the warm sofa. The rest went something like this:

"Okay into the car everybody."

"Children! Less noise, please!"

"Well, make up your mind. What flavor do you want?"

"Watch it! It's melting all over the car seat!"

"So they didn't have the flavor you like. Do you have to be such babies about it?"

"There will be no seconds! In fact there will be nothing for a long time."

The "treat" ended with a chorus of caterwauling.

What had happened?

I had put aside my paper and set out to be "nice," to make everybody happy, and had wound up making everyone cry. Obviously I had misjudged my feelings. I thought I was feeling "nice." Maybe I really had been feeling resentful———I didn't know what I felt.

Think of it! What person engaged in demanding work

could afford to ignore his genuine feelings? A surgeon wouldn't yield to pressure to be a "nice guy" and do a few more operations a day. It wouldn't be safe for his patients. A tightrope walker wouldn't venture forth on a wire that felt shaky. It could be his last walk. No truck driver would keep driving all night if he felt his eyelids getting heavy. He might never reach his destination. Yet here I was with the most demanding job of all—the rearing of human beings—ignoring my feelings over and over again as if there would be no consequences.

How had I gotten so out of touch with myself where my children were concerned? Why was I constantly tripped up by acting one way when I really felt another? What was getting in my way?

I thought about my parents. They had never seemed at all confused. They knew exactly what they felt where their children were concerned. I had heard it all a hundred times:

"The children are our lives."

"Their health and happiness are what we care about most."

"No sacrifice on our part is too great for them."

Theirs was a life of complete devotion: It was "the children," first, last, and always.

How did I feel about all this? I rejected it, of course! I was the modern mother, searching for new ways. I had outgrown those old-fashioned, self-sacrificing, narrow notions. Or had I? Then why was I so uncomfortable when certain thoughts (thoughts my parents would have regarded with horror) pushed their way into my consciousness:

"I want a life of my own, apart from the kids."

"Raising humane humans may be a lofty goal—but sometimes I hardly care."

"I'm locked in by the daily routine—and the kids are still so young; I've got years ahead of me."

"Sometimes I don't even like my own children."

When I juxtaposed these thoughts against my parents' *Alles fur die Kinder* philosophy, I felt like some kind of monster. And the mass media did little to improve my self-esteem. Radio, TV, and magazines all beamed a different set of messages to parents that were equally unnerving:

Raising children should be a natural, spontaneous, joyful experience. (Oh, there are those trying times, but with a little humor we can weather the storms.)

One must learn how to relax. Relaxed parents make for relaxed children.

All a parent needs is to *be more:* more flexible, more imaginative, more understanding, more playful, more resourceful.

And to *do more!* Take the children on outings. Provide them with creative toys. Play with them for fun and to raise their IQ's. Surprise them with home-baked delights in their lunch boxes. Become a den mother. A community leader. Be a model parent for your child to emulate. Be a supermother!

These words of wisdom must have been addressed to some paragon, a combination of Mary Poppins, Joan of Arc, and Florence Nightingale. No ordinary mortal could possibly live up to such standards.

It suddenly occurred to me. There was a startling similarity between the mandates of the past generation and those of the present. They both demanded a degree of selflessness that seemed appropriate for either saints or martyrs. But at least in the past, one was entitled to one's martyrdom. Today, we're expected to give much more, do much more—and *smile.* In neither generation is there room for negative thoughts. And the discrepancy between what I really *did* feel and what I had been told I *ought* to feel gave me the sensation of being caught in a vise.

Dr. Ginott had often said, "Parents operate on unnecessary guilt." My guilt may have been unnecessary, but it certainly was there—goading me into acting nicer than I felt; making me give when I had nothing left to give; urging me to push myself beyond my limits; and seldom allowing me the luxury of my own real feelings.

An astonishing thought occurred to me. I had permitted the children *their* feelings—even the negative ones. Could I, as an adult, give myself the same kind of permission in this highly-charged area and still feel like a good parent? The thought excited me. I felt I had come upon something important.

When I told the group what was on my mind, I touched a responsive chord. They seemed to catch my excitement, and together we started to explore these ideas. Our discussions must have had some impact because the following week a number of stories came back that had a new element.

When it was my turn, I announced, "I wish to report a first! I was on my way home from a long series of errands—all for David. It was late and cold and my thoughts were racing ahead as to how I could put together a fast supper. My coat was still on when David asked for soup. I hadn't planned to serve soup, but I automatically started looking for a can in the pantry, thinking, 'Why not? How could a loving mother deny her son hot soup on a cold night?' Then I thought about our discussion last week, and it hit me that I didn't really feel loving—I *really felt put-upon!* At that moment finding the can, opening it, and having an extra pot to wash seemed like a big imposition. I said, 'David, no soup! I feel pressured. What I could use is some help. Would you peel the carrots, please?'

"Do you know what happened? Just as I thought I would be struck by lightning, David said, 'O.K. How many do you need?' But that's not all. The next night he came into the kitchen, looked into my face and said, 'Mom, are you in a good mood tonight? Do you think you'd mind making soup?'

"*Mind?* I was so touched that my son was interested in how *I* felt for a change, I heard myself answer, 'What kind would you like, David?' "

Dr. Ginott commented, "You gave your son something more important than hot soup. You gave him your honest feelings, and you gave him an opportunity to take another person's needs into consideration."

The group beamed their approval at me. All except Katherine. She looked uncomfortable. "I can't really identify with this story. I guess it's because I grew up in the kind of home where the adults came first. In my parents' home it wouldn't be *suggested* that the children peel the carrots; it would be *expected*. And no child would think of asking for anything extra. We knew we had to eat what was served to us. So this situation would have been no problem for me. I could easily have said, 'No soup, dear,' and I wouldn't have felt the need to explain why either."

I listened to Katherine and thought to myself, "It's so easy for her! What I'm struggling to make part of me, she knows in her bones." And I suspected that for me, no matter how much I tried, it would always be a fight; I would always be working against my natural tendency to put myself last.

Roslyn spoke up. "Now the situation with the soup wouldn't be a problem for me either. I don't find it hard to go along with my feelings when I think I'm entitled to them. And Jan was certainly entitled in her case. She was under pressure to get dinner ready quickly. She had every reason to feel the way she did."

Dr. Ginott interrupted. "*Roslyn, a person does not need a reason to feel what he feels. The fact that he feels it, is reality enough.*"

Roslyn continued as if she hadn't heard his words at all. "For example, the other afternoon I felt very tired. I had had a good night's sleep. There was no reason to be tired, so when the kids begged to go ice-skating after school, I pushed myself and took them."

Dr. Ginott answered, "Roslyn, a parent is not to be pushed —even by herself. You would have done yourself and your children a greater service had you said, 'Children, your mother feels tired. I'm going into my room for a half hour to restore my energy. I know you'll be able to figure out some quiet activity while I'm resting.' And then Roslyn, you could go into your room and hang a 'Do not disturb' sign on the door."

A general sigh was heard in the room. I, too, felt a great sense of relief. If Dr. Ginott was giving Roslyn permission for all her feelings, then I would give myself permission for all of mine.

During the next few days, I became very "feeling-oriented." At first certain feelings seemed vague, elusive; they wouldn't be pinned down. Then little by little I became more adept at forcing some of these blurred feelings into sharper focus. On Saturday, for example, everyone was pulling at me, each one wanting something else. Instead of automatically "doing for," I stopped and asked myself, "What are you really feeling now, Janet? No excuses, no apologies—out with it!"

I answered myself slowly:

"I feel like a stretched-out piece of elastic—no give."

"I feel as if I couldn't stand even one more 'take me, get me, or give me.' "

"I feel like slapping each one of them across their loud, demanding, mouths."

To the children I said, "I hear requests for a lot of different things. But right now there is something *I* have to take care of. When I return, we'll discuss what's on your mind." Then I put on my coat and walked out the door.

All I did was walk around the block, and yet I felt surprisingly light-hearted. I could even enjoy the mean little satisfaction of having pulled the rug out from under them. There was a real release in being able to own up to one's worst! And there was a feeling of strength that came from knowing that the worst isn't permanent—that just feeling the worst doesn't mean you have to act it out. The fact is, I hadn't slapped them.

I described the experience to the group. Lee was skeptical. "Fine," she said, "you were able to do something about your negative feelings. But what's the good of finding out what you feel when you *can't* do anything about it? All right, so I admit to myself that at times I feel very resentful toward my children. A lot of good it does! I come home from marketing with eight heavy bundles and call out for help. Somebody yells, 'I'll be right down. Mom.' I wait and nobody shows.

"Before, I used to make excuses for them. 'Oh well, they're just kids.' But now I'm very clear on the fact that I feel resentful at having to beg for help. I'd like help to be offered willingly.

"I call up again, 'I'm waiting. The ice cream is melting!' When I hear, 'Just a minute, Mom!' I say to myself, 'The heck with them all!' and carry the bundles in myself. And for the rest of the evening I'm steaming inside. . . . My point is, Dr. Ginott, I have doubts that just knowing how you feel can automatically lead to a solution."

Dr. Ginott answered, "Lee, your doubts are justified. There are times when we know our feelings and still can't do anything about them. And, as adults, we also know that there are certain feelings that are best left unexpressed. Chances are you wouldn't say to an attractive man at a cocktail party, 'I've been watching you and thinking what a wonderful lover you'd make.' You might very well feel that way, but you wouldn't necessarily express the thought.

"However in the situation you describe, Lee, I think it *would* be helpful if your family knew how you felt. You could say to your children just what you said to me: 'When I ask for help and don't get it, I feel resentful. . . . I like help to be offered willingly. . . . When I carry the bundles in myself, I steam inside!' Then if you still don't get help, you can announce in a loud voice, 'I am carrying the bundles in myself, and now you have a resentful mother!' Your children will have to notice that there are unpleasant consequences when they ignore a request for help."

The group decided that at this time we would not linger on those feelings that could not be expressed, or those problems that had no solutions. Our concentration had to be directed toward those feelings, those situations where some answers— even partial ones—could be found.

For myself, I was becoming very skillful at nailing one particular feeling that I had previously pushed aside. I could best describe it as a kind of tight, visceral sensation. It usually came when I had to make a quick decision about something for which I had no quick answer. Now, when I felt the knot in my stomach, I responded to it as if a red light were signaling: "Stop! You're feeling conflicted. Something is disturbing you so much your innards ache. You need time—time for thinking through—time for separating the important from the unimportant." I found that when I did take the time, I operated from a position of greater strength.

I told the group about my experience with Andy when he asked me to be class mother. He had made the same request for the last three years—and with each year my apologies had grown more elaborate. This time I didn't have an excuse left. I was about to say yes when the knot stopped me. I said, 'Andy, I need time to think about it. I'll have an answer for you after supper.' For the next hour I turned it over in my mind. How did I really feel about being class mother?

"I hate the very thought of it."

"I feel bad about refusing."

"What's the matter with me? Other women take the job without making such a big deal of it."

"But the phone calls, collecting class money, planning parties, pressuring people to volunteer."

"I REALLY DON'T WANT TO!"

"When Andy came to me after supper, I was ready. 'Andy, I've given very serious thought to your request because I know how much it means to you. Honey, the answer is no. Being class mother is not for me. But here's what I'd like to do. I'd really enjoy being with you on a field trip. If it's all right with you, I'll call the teacher and ask her to put my name on the top of the list for the next field trip.' "

Dr. Ginott commented. "Children are masters at throwing us off balance. They ask all kinds of questions for which they want immediate answers: 'Mother, can we have a dog?' 'Daddy, can I have a new bicycle?' We're not computers that can discharge instant answers. When we take the time to clarify our feelings, we often find that we're not as boxed-in as we thought we were. With reflection comes new possibilities.

"Notice what else happens when we think a decision through. Our responses to the children take on an entirely different quality. Instead of saying 'Yes' angrily, we say it graciously. Even our 'No' comes out simply and nondefensively, with genuine concern for the child's feelings.

"There was one aspect of your story, however, that bothered me, Jan. It was when you asked yourself, 'What's the matter with me? Why can't I be like the other mothers?' A question like that only confuses. It presupposes that we *should* feel like other people. But we don't. We're *not* other people. We're ourselves. You are *you*. We come back to the same thing again. We can only feel what we feel.

"And we really do feel very differently—each of us does—not only about being class mother, but about everything. One mother loves to bake with her children, and another can't stand having them underfoot in the kitchen; one loves gathering the little ones around to read aloud, another shudders at the thought. We each have our strengths and our limitations. And part of maturity is learning to make friends with our very human limitations."

You could have heard a pin drop. Each woman had turned inward to locate her particular "limitation." Could she really make friends with it? Could she even own up to it?

Evelyn broke the silence. "I'll tell you what I feel awful about. It's my children telling me I'm not a playful mother. And do you know what? I'm not. My teeth go on edge every time one of them comes at me with the checker set or a deck of cards. I really don't enjoy playing games."

"But do you anyway?" Roslyn asked.

"Well . . . yes," Evelyn replied, "when I have the time. I mean . . . isn't a child entitled to have his mother play with him?"

"Evelyn," said Dr. Ginott, "where is it written that a mother must play cards with her child? Tell me, have you read all the books you'd like to read, or heard all the music you'd like to hear?"

Evelyn's mouth fell open. "Do you mean," she exclaimed, "that I've been playing War, Go Fish, and Old Maid all these years—and it wasn't even necessary!"

"But Dr. Ginott," Roslyn protested, "I enjoy playing cards with my children. It's just about the only activity we can all do together without fighting. Are you saying that I shouldn't?"

"I'm saying," answered Dr. Ginott, "that it's essential to operate in a way that's consistent with our real feelings. If playing games sets Evelyn's teeth on edge, then she's better off refusing because while she's playing War, she might start a little war of her own. On the other hand, if a game is a happy experience for a parent, then it's likely to be pleasurable for everyone.

"Children need responses that are genuine. If our words say one thing, and our gestures and tone of voice say another, we can literally drive them crazy."

"But suppose," Roslyn said in a troubled voice, "your genuine response is unhelpful to your child? For instance, I hate driving, but in suburbia it's an absolute necessity. Amy has to be driven to friends, the library, her piano lessons, scout meetings, the orthodontist. Half my day is spent either picking her up or delivering. Now I can't see taking out my resentment on Amy. There's nothing she can do about it. So I say, 'Hop in, honey!' with all the cheerfulness I can muster."

"I'd be interested in seeing your cheerful greeting," said Dr. Ginott. "Somehow I suspect that while your mouth is smiling, your eye is twitching. Roslyn, do you really believe that your daughter isn't aware that you're irritated? I assure you, she is. I can also assure you that she can cope more easily with your honest emotion than with a phony smile."

"Are you suggesting that I tell her she's a royal pain in the neck and refuse to drive her?"

"I'm suggesting," said Dr. Ginott, "that when there is a tense situation, it's a good idea for the parent to ask himself, 'Who has the problem?' If the child has the problem, the child speaks. If the parent has the problem, the parent speaks. He speaks about himself and his feelings. He doesn't blame or accuse. The key word is 'I.'

"In your case, Roslyn, you might say, 'Amy, I have a problem. Some people enjoy driving. I hate it. Every time I have to drive, I say to myself, "Now I have to interrupt what I'm doing, get my coat, go out into the cold, struggle with the garage door, hunt for my keys, try to get the car started. Just thinking about driving makes me feel disagreeable!" '

"Now what happens? Amy has to cope with your low tolerance for driving. Perhaps her friends could visit her more often. Perhaps she could walk to the library or her scout meetings. Walking is fine exercise. Whenever possible her bicycle could become her transportation. Roslyn, it won't end all your driving, but it will reduce it. And Amy, knowing how hard it is for you to drive, might begin to ask in a different way: 'Mom, would you mind . . .' Even that might lessen your resentment. But, most important, your daughter will have heard her mother's honest feelings instead of a confusing double message."

I listened and thought, "I must have come a long way."

A short time ago I might have said to myself, "Maybe that's all right for Roslyn, but not for me. My child shouldn't have to put up with my real feelings or my limitations. I should rise above them. Anything else would be irresponsible. Why a parent's first obligation is to the children!"

Not so. A parent has another first obligation: to herself. To *her* needs, *her* feelings, even to her "limitations."

Those original words of Dr. Ginott that I had so grudgingly copied into my notebook suddenly seemed very friendly, brimful of meaning, relevant.

A parent should respect his own limits.

We can be a little nicer than we feel, but not much.

It is important to accept the reality of our feelings of the moment.

It's best to be authentic with our children.

Chapter X

Protection—for Me, for Them,
for All of Us

Six months had passed. Strange to think that I had once doubted the importance of my own feelings. These days I almost automatically consulted them, and each time it became a little easier.

Now when I slipped back to my old ways (and I still did), it was with a difference. A part of me coolly watched the mechanics of what was taking place. It seemed to me that whenever I ignored my feelings, an almost diabolical set of dynamics would swing into motion.

The sequence was as follows:

1. The children make demands.
2. Mother ignores her negative feelings and complies.
3. Resentment creeps in.
4. Resentment comes out.
5. Someone gets hurt.
6. The whole family suffers.

Each time the pattern would repeat itself.

The time I made myself endure David's "creative" banging

on the piano despite my headache. Then, one hour later snapping at everyone and sending David to bed early, confused and in tears.

The time I let Jill nag me into buying her a pair of shoes she really didn't need. The long, angry lecture I delivered on the way home about the evils of extravagance. Jill coming into the house sullen, hostile, making fun of her brother.

And it seemed the same for Ted, too. The time he canceled his fishing trip to take the kids to an amusement park. Andy's complaining that Ted was "mean" not to allow another ride on the roller-coaster. Ted's hand slapping Andy with unexpected force. Andy's scream. Me, angry at Ted for over-reacting. Jill asking us if we were going to get a divorce.

From experiences like these came a deep conviction: If a parent's feelings control the great gears of family life, then these feelings must be protected. If a mother or father is pushed beyond endurance, full of resentment, out of control, then the best of situations can turn sour and the worst become nightmarish. But if mother or father feels calm, stable, under control, full of good will, almost anything can be borne, coped with, handled, lived through, and even laughed at. The children are safe. They are in good hands.

And so I strove to learn better how to protect myself—how to stand guard over my good will. For the welfare of all of us, I would try to tune in carefully to what I really felt; try not to give too much, lest I forfeit my control; be almost stingy at times, so that I might be more generous later on; protect the core of my equanimity as a source of my own strength—as a source of strength for each member of my family.

I had a new respect for my own worth. I likened myself to a fine piece of machinery performing a vital function: a complex, delicate instrument that was to be handled with care and kept in peak condition.

No. More than that. I was the Queen Bee: the nerve center

upon which the whole colony depended; the force that held the life of the hive together. And woe betide us all if the Queen's needs are ignored!

Just entertaining these kinds of thoughts began to affect my behavior. In the past when I had focused on my own needs, it was with a spirit of defiance—a spirit of "I'm a person too. I also have rights." Now when I protected myself I felt a quiet certitude. What I was doing was for me, for them, for all of us.

I noticed that my old way of explaining myself almost with embarrassment was disappearing. It used to be, "I'm so sorry honey. I know I said I'd take you for a new baseball mitt this afternoon, but I've been doing closets all day and I'm pooped. Let me lie down for a while, and see how I feel, O.K.?"

Imagine! A grown woman saying" let me" to a child.

Imagine! A mother asking her child's permission to lie down before she drops down.

Imagine an adult putting her welfare in the hands of a child! I confess, however, that even this was progress. There was a time when if I said I would go, I went—tired or not. What else would a "good mother" do?

I looked back at both these stages, thankful that they were behind me. I was on a different level now. My new watchwords became:

"Explanations are unseemly."

"Apologies are inappropriate."

"Protection for my family begins with self-protection."

These days I would say, "Honey, I have a disappointment for both of us. I had planned to take you for your new mitt today, and now I see that I can't. Hopefully, I'll be free Friday or Saturday afternoon. Which would be better for you?" And if outraged wails of protest arose, I wouldn't go under with doubts. I'd simply repeat quietly, "Friday or Saturday afternoon." One more wail and I'd leave the room. A parent was not to be shrieked at.

And there was yet another way that I was learning to protect myself—not just from their demands, but from their moods. Just because Andy was dejected about having no one to play with for the afternoon didn't mean that I had to share his misery. Just because Jill was almost twitching with fear over a unit test didn't mean that I had to twitch along with her.

Dr. Ginott had often pointed out that it was in the interest of a parent's mental health not to be infected by his child's moods. He'd say, "A doctor would be of little use to his patient if he were to catch his every illness."

My parents could never have understood this. They would have been ashamed to smile when we were unhappy. To them it would have been a sign that they didn't care. A *real* parent suffered along with his children.

I was so glad to be free of that burdensome attitude. When David went to pieces about not being chosen for the school orchestra, I listened and gently empathized. Then at one point it started to get to me. I stood up to go and said, "Well, I have to get ready to leave now. Daddy and I have theater tickets tonight."

David looked startled. "How can you be so cheerful," he asked, "when I'm so miserable?"

I thought about that. "It's because, David, you're a person and I'm a person. And we both have different feelings. But I understand that you're suffering."

Not only did I say the words, but I think I meant them! There was only one thing that kept me from crowing over myself. It was the memory of the last time Ted and I had theater tickets. David had a problem that night, too; but instead of knowing enough to leave it home, I brought it along for the evening. Together, Ted and I would get to the bottom of this! Together, we would agonize over our child's agony! Poor Ted. I outlined the problem for him during dinner; presented him with two possible solutions before the curtain rose;

and demanded his reactions to both of them during intermissions. The play was a comedy, but neither of us laughed much. By the time the curtain came down, Ted couldn't look at me.

Tonight would be different. Tonight, I would leave David's problem home with David, and enjoy an evening out with my husband.

And then there was the other side of the coin. Occasionally the children needed protection from *me*—from *my* moods. A month ago a dear friend was in critical condition after a car accident. I didn't want to upset the children, so I tried to go about the day in my usual way.

But there was nothing usual about my behavior. The children spoke to me and I didn't hear them. Even when I tried to listen, my mind would drift. A few minutes later I'd suddenly find myself yelling over a sofa pillow that was out of place. It occurred to me after a while, looking at their bewildered faces, that maybe the children *should* know something.

I called them into my room and groped for the words. "Kids," I said "you may have noticed that I've been sort of jumpy and faraway lately . . . probably not very easy to talk to. Now I want you to know that it has nothing to do with you —nothing at all. It's because of something that's on my mind."

I didn't dare say anything more because my voice was beginning to quaver. I left the room wondering whether they had even understood me. No, they hadn't, I decided when Andy came in a minute later in hysterics. Someone had "stolen" his new red pen.

I thought, "What'll I do? I don't have the strength to cope with it now." From nowhere David appeared. He put his arm around Andy and softly said, "Don't bother Mom now. Come on, I'll help you find your pen."

I thought, "How dear of him! He *had* heard me. I wished I

had spoken up sooner. Maybe next time I'd be able to move in more swiftly. Maybe next time I would even be able to warn the family about my mood *in advance* so that they could take cover before the storm broke."

The next time was Thanksgiving Day. I woke up that morning and looked at Ted sleeping peacefully. "Lucky," I thought, "he's not worrying about twenty-two relatives descending upon him before the beds are made, the table set, or the rings removed from the bath tub."

A year ago I would have felt the need to suppress my panic and play the magazine mother—smiling in a flowered apron, basting the turkey with one hand while helping Jill stir the cranberry mold with the other. (It was important that the children feel they were participating.)

Today my only thought was "How do I keep my cool?" I threw on my old jeans, went into the kitchen, and dug in. I had a fistful of stuffing in my hand and was heading toward the turkey when Andy and David appeared at the door. Andy screamed, "Don't put it in—let me!" David shoved him and shouted, "You did it last year. It's my turn!"

There wasn't a minute to lose. The Queen was in danger! The enemy was within. The whole hive was threatened! I summoned up all available reserves for defense. I announced, "Listen, you two. I'm mad as a hornet. The least little thing will make me zoom and sting! And I don't want anyone to get hurt."

David said, "Can I stay if I'm quiet and only do what you say to do?"

"Yes, but if you're not feeling supercooperative, then clear out. Because it's not safe around here!"

The challenge was too much for Andy. He *had* to try me out. "But you promised I could do it again this year!" With the stuffing still on my hands, I grabbed him by the shoulders, spun him toward the door, said "OUT!" and escorted the little saboteur from the room.

It was bracing. What power to be so in touch with my own feelings that I could give myself *and* my family the protection we needed when we needed it!

Jill came home from school with a funny smile on her face. I said, "Hey there, something's tickling you."

"Well," she said, "you know Robin, she thinks she's so great. She always cuts in front of me on the lunch line and says, 'Oh Jill, you don't mind if I get in front of you, do you? Please, I'll be your best friend.' I always let her, even though I don't want to—and then she doesn't even talk to me! She just starts calling all her friends into the line in front of her.

"But today, you know what I said? I said, 'No Robin, I decided I don't like it when you cut in on me.' And you know what she did? She went to the end of the line."

I was amazed. This "rotten Robin" had been pushing my kid around since the beginning of the term. Where did Jill get the nerve and the know-how to stand up for herself?

I knew the answer. It was from me! And though it could never be proved scientifically, I was unshakable. She had learned it from me! All those months of insisting upon the importance of *my* feelings had been a model for my daughter. From my new-found strength Jill had learned what a thousand lectures could not have taught her.

In the midst of my maternal pride, I experienced a twinge of envy. Jill knew at eight what it had taken me half a lifetime to learn.

Chapter XI
Guilt and Suffering

During all those sessions in which we explored parents' feelings and the means of protecting them, Katherine had sat silently. But there was no mistaking the disapproval etched upon her tightly pressed lips. Finally one day she exploded.

"Dr. Ginott, we've been talking about parents' feelings as if they existed in a vacuum! Our children have no one to depend upon except us! Can parents be so self-indulgent that they stop doing for a child? A child is at our mercy. We can't just give in to our every feeling! Why, if a mother followed her real feelings, she'd stay in bed till noon, never change the baby's diaper, and stick a lollipop in his mouth every time he cried—just because she has a low tolerance for noise! If a parent won't take care of a child's needs, then who will?"

"Katherine," said Dr. Ginott, "Your concern is valid. It is a parent's obligation to take care of a child's real needs, especially in the early years. A mother may want a good night's sleep, but she can't have it. The baby needs a two A.M. bottle. If a little toddler is exhausted, he needs to be carried.

"But, as a child matures, he no longer requires instant satisfaction of his needs. It isn't even good for him. As parents, it's our job to start teaching him, little by little, how to postpone some of his needs. This helps him grow. For example, a five-year-old can be helped to put off his need to go to the bathroom while his mother is waiting in line for her change at the supermarket. She whispers, 'It's hard to wait when you have to go so badly. As soon as I get my change, we'll make a beeline for the bathroom.' His mother teaches him to endure temporary discomfort out of deference to the feelings of those around him. We don't want our children to remain emotionally infantile. We'd like them to be able to take the feelings of others into consideration."

Nell seemed distressed. "But Dr. Ginott," she said, "what do you do when you have a conflict between a child's needs and a parent's needs? I mean . . . well, as you know, Kenneth has practically no friends. Most of his days are pretty lonely. Yesterday a neighbor came over with a puppy that she couldn't keep any longer and asked if we wanted it. You should have seen Kenneth. He fell to his knees, and there was a look on his face while he held that dog that I had never seen before. He brushed his cheek against the puppy's fur and then looked up and said, 'Can we keep it? Oh, please, Mom, can we?'

I wanted so much to give it to him. It was an adorable puppy, and I knew what it would mean to Kenneth. But Dr. Ginott, I'm allergic to animal fur. It makes me cough. I just don't know what to do at this point. His need is so great. I think I'm just going to let him have it."

Very gently Dr. Ginott said, "Nell, *a child's pleasure should not come at the price of a parent's suffering.* The cost is too great for both. The parent pays with his health and his goodwill, and the child pays in another way.

"What does a child say to himself when he gets something

at his parent's expense? He says, 'I made my mother get me a puppy. My mother is coughing and getting sick because of me. I'm a terrible person. I'm scared!'

"Nell, when children see us suffer on their account, they automatically feel responsible. Our suffering gives them guilt and fear.

"Now let's get back to your original statement about a conflict of needs. Whenever I hear about a child needing something, I ask myself, 'Is it what he *needs* or what he *wants?*' It isn't always easy to distinguish between the two. A child has many real needs which can and should be satisfied. His *wants* are a bottomless pit. He wants, for example, to sleep with his parents. He needs to be in his own bed. At Christmas he wants every toy advertised on television. He needs only one or two.

"Now what about Kenneth's case? What does he want? He wants a dog. Nell, what does he *need?*"

Nell thought a while. Tentatively she said, "I guess what he really needs is a friend."

"And all he needs from you," Dr. Ginott said, "is your support while he's finding and making a friend." Then he turned to the group. "When you permit a child to see you suffer on his account, you do him no favor. You teach him, by your example, how *not* to protect himself. You teach him how to operate from weakness instead of strength."

I listened intently. What Dr. Ginott was describing, the "loving suffering" of parents for children, had been a normal part of my growing years. And not mine alone! I could have dropped in on almost any home of any ethnic group in the neighborhood and heard:

"You take the heart out of me. You know how I worry myself sick whenever you go there. Oh, if it's that important to you—go!"

"You eat the rest of the meat, sweetheart. You're a growing

boy. Never mind about me. I'll make do with something else."

"Don't worry about your tuition, son. If I have to work over-time, then I will. You just stick to the studying."

The only payment these parents wanted was the child's love and gratitude. But their children didn't feel grateful. They felt hateful. The parents were willing to give their all: their pain, their suffering, their sacrifice—and their children were choking on it.

I made a mental note to be wary. Any suffering I endured on my children's account should be none of their business. I'd try to do things for them willingly, with no strings—or not at all. I could see where it would be better to give nothing than to give a load of guilt.

At the next session it was Roslyn who came in with a problem. "I don't even know why I should be so upset, but I am. Peter woke up late this morning, was rushing to get out, and couldn't find any socks. I turned pale when he asked me for them because I knew the whole load of wash was soaking wet in the machine. I immediately said, 'Peter, I have a solution. You can borrow a pair of Daddy's socks.'

"He started to carry on about how I never have the laundry ready on time, and how he couldn't depend upon me for any-thing. I tried to explain how busy I'd been lately, but he just wouldn't listen. Finally he stormed out of the house—late and *without socks*. I felt like an unfit mother."

Dr. Ginott smiled ruefully. "It doesn't take much to stir up a parent's guilt, does it? But to let a child know that he has the power to make us feel guilty is not helpful to him. The child suddenly assumes the role of prosecuting attorney while the parent cringes on the witness stand. When a child is permitted to do this to his parent, how do you think he feels about him-self?''

Roslyn thought a while. Then she ventured, "Guilty . . . frightened . . . like he's an awful person."

"All of that," said Dr. Ginott.

Roslyn sighed deeply. "And I really thought I was helping him! . . . But I still don't see what else I could have done."

"We talked before about a child's real needs," said Dr. Ginott. "What Peter needed this morning wasn't a guilty explanation or an instant solution. He needed the opportunity to exercise his autonomy, his own initiative. He needed to solve his own problem.

"Now how do we help him with his real needs? First of all, if he has to worry about whom to blame, he can't think con-structively. Accusations and counteraccusations will only get in his way. We can ease him over the whose-fault-is-it? hurdle by a statement like, 'Son, the responsibility for having clean socks ready is mine.' This leaves Peter more free to think in terms of solutions.

"Second, we help him by acknowledging the difficulty of his problem. You might say to him, 'What does one do in a case like this? There isn't a dry pair of socks in the house. That's what I call a real dilemma!' By describing his problem seri-ously, we show that whatever it is that's troubling him is worthy of respect.

"Then, Roslyn, comes the hardest part of all. Say to yourself, *'Don't just do something; stand there.'* You see, it's the parent's willingness to stand by silently while the child himself works out his own solution that is the greatest help."

Helen waved her hand. "I've got the mate to Roslyn's ex-perience. In fact, I'm right in the middle of it. Today is the day of the school picnic. Laurie had reminded me to please buy a canned drink, tuna fish, and a cupcake. Well, I forgot. I was so busy chiseling my new sculpture, *Mother and Child,* that I neglected my own child. This morning when Laurie opened the refrigerator door, she turned pale.

" 'Mommy,' she cried, 'there's only bread, mayonnaise, ketchup, mustard, and a can of cat food. What can I make with that?'

"You can imagine how I felt! But I was determined not to let Laurie know. I said, 'Honey, it was my job to buy your picnic food and somehow I forgot. This is a predicament. Even if you scrounged around I don't know what you could come up with.'

"Well scrounge she did, and finally she located a nearly empty jar of oily peanut butter. Very quickly she spread it on two slices of stale bread, all the while mumbling to herself about how there wasn't even dessert. Then she ran upstairs. When she returned to the kitchen, she triumphantly held one lemon lollipop and said, 'Look what I found! It was left over from Halloween!'

"Wasn't that plucky? And I *did* help her, didn't I? I mean, I didn't give her my guilt, and I got her to focus on solutions to the problem—so I ought to feel good. . . . I feel awful. I can just picture her sitting there with that pathetic lunch while the other kids are gorging themselves on goodies prepared for them, in advance, by their responsible mothers. I probably ruined her whole day. I don't even know what to say to her when she comes home this afternoon. Maybe I'll just tell her how sorry I am, and somehow try to make amends."

"Helen," said Dr. Ginott, "as parents we won't be able to keep ourselves from having guilty feelings, but we can say to ourselves, 'I must not permit my child to know of them; it's too dangerous—for everyone.' When a child is given the power to activate our guilt, it's like handing him an atomic bomb. As Roslyn pointed out, the child who stirs up a parent's guilt, feels guilty about what he's done. And do you know the emotion we ultimately experience toward people who make us feel guilty? It's hatred. When we permit guilt, we invite hatred."

These words seemed to have touched a live nerve in Lee. "It's true!" she cried. "You *can* get to hate people who make you feel guilty! I've always been so fond of my mother-in-law. She's a big, hearty, independent woman. But lately I don't know what's happened to her. She's become a master at injecting guilt. Oh, she'll never accuse me of anything outright, mind you. But she'll say things like, 'You knew I went to the doctor, dear. I thought I'd hear from you.' Or, 'I'd love to spend more time with you, Lee, but I know how busy you are and I try to understand.'

"I suppose it isn't very nice of me, but I find myself avoiding her these days. Whenever she's around, every other word out of my mouth is an apology. It's gotten so I even dread her phone calls. You know, I never thought about it before, but guilt is sort of like a poison—isn't it? You can't see it, you can't smell it, but once it enters a relationship, everything that's been warm and friendly between two people slowly shrivels up and dies."

Helen, whose eyes were riveted on Lee, leaned forward in her seat. "Poison is the right word!" she exclaimed. "And it's not only fatal to a relationship, but even a small dose of it can alter your *own* personality. You suddenly find that you're saying and doing things that make you a stranger to yourself. Take this morning, for instance. I felt so guilty after Laurie left that all I could think about was how to apologize to her when she came home. I was in such bad shape that had she called me 'disorganized' or 'neglectful,' I probably would have agreed with her. Now that's not like me!"

Helen turned to Dr. Ginott. "And can you see where that

would have led? I would have resented her for making me feel guilty. She would have hated *herself* for having *made* me feel guilty. And both of us would have wound up resenting each other. Well, there will be no apologies when she comes home this afternoon! In fact if she dares to open her mouth to accuse me, I just might hit her."

Everyone laughed.

"It's not so funny," Helen said. "I still don't know what to say to her when she comes home this afternoon."

"In the first place," said Dr. Ginott, "don't *you* be the one to bring up the subject. Very often what was a crisis in the morning has been resolved by the afternoon. It's even possible that the tragedy could have turned into a triumph: She could have traded her lollipop for a chicken leg. Or, another child could have offered to share her juice with Laurie. Maybe a new friendship was started!

"In the second place, Helen, our alternatives are not so harsh. We have a whole range of responses at our disposal that are more effective than either hitting or apologizing. For example, we can say any of the following, depending upon our mood:

" 'Laurie, that is not a good way to approach me. I don't like it when I am attacked.'

" 'Laurie, when I am called names, I can't be helpful. In fact, I can't even listen.'

" 'No accusations, Laurie! If you have any recommendations, put them in writing in a way that will enable me to consider them!'

" 'Honey, talk to me about *your* disappointment, *your* irritation, *your* feelings. Then I'll know what they are and I'll be able to respond.'

"You see, Helen, we have many ways to disarm our children and teach them, at the same time, how to approach us with a complaint. Tell me, does what I'm saying now make sense to you?"

Helen looked up from her notebook. "I'm writing as fast as you're talking," she smiled. "And what's more, I guarantee that one of those statements will be put to use before the day is over. I think what pleases me most is the idea of not having to be a willing victim when an eight-year-old comes at me. But . . . " and here she stopped.

"Something still bothers you?"

"Yes, it does! The fact is, I *should* have had things prepared for her today, and it just eats at me that I didn't."

"Now," said Dr. Ginott, "the question is: What does one do with one's guilty feelings? Again, Helen, there are alternatives. We can talk to others—to a friend, a husband, our group here, a minister, a rabbi, a priest, a therapist—anyone who will lend an ear without sitting in judgment.

"And we can talk to ourselves. We can tell ourselves, 'I can work out my guilt without my children's help. I don't need absolution from them. I don't need 'I forgive you, Mommy' from a little child. For me it is enough that *I* decide to do better next time.' "

Evelyn looked uncertain. "I don't know if I quite understand it all yet, Dr. Ginott. Something occurred a while back that I'm still wondering about. I'd be interested in your reaction. I'm thinking of the night that my husband, Marty, got up from his reading chair to take a drink. The second he left, my two boys pounced on the chair. When Marty returned the boys refused to give him his chair back. They didn't see why they had to. 'Why should a Daddy always have the best chair? Just because he's older? It's not fair! Children have rights too!'

"I remember thinking, 'Gee, they have a point there. It really is the only comfortable chair. Then I heard Marty answer as he pulled them off, 'There are certain privileges that come with age. And when you become a parent you'll get them from your children!' The boys just blinked. Then Marty settled back in his chair and said, 'And if you don't, I'll tell you what to do!' Both boys leaned forward. 'Demand it!' said Marty, 'and you'll get it!'

"It seemed to me that Marty was being a little harsh with the boys, but now I'm not so sure."

Dr. Ginott asked, "How do you feel about it now?"

"I think maybe he did the right thing after all," Evelyn answered. "According to what you've been saying, if Marty had let the children make him feel guilty about sitting in his own chair, it wouldn't have been good for the children."

Dr. Ginott nodded. "Your husband taught your children a valuable lesson. It's important that we all understand that as parents we owe our children no explanation for our actions. That doesn't mean the children won't try to trap us into a guilty response. But it's best that we follow Marty's example and not nibble at the bait. They ask, 'Why do you go on vacations alone? Why don't you take us?' Or, 'Why doesn't mother go back to work? Then we'd all have more money.' Or, 'Why can't I have a new camera? You just bought a new car.'

"We must not be drawn into explanations or defense— even in these vulnerable moments. As parents we have to make certain decisions that represent our best adult judgment at the time. And the decision-making process does not necessarily have to be shared with our children; nor do we permit their evaluation. We can say to them, 'I hear you. But that's not your concern. These things are for Mommy and Daddy to decide.' When a parent is clear about his rights, when he knows that guilt is an inappropriate response, then he helps his child gather strength and learn reality."

I thought about the session all the way home. Do we really strengthen a child by not sharing our guilt with him? I remembered an incident many winters ago. It was snowing and David asked me to drive him five blocks to kindergarten. But it was just too hard to pack up the two younger ones, so I told him he'd have to manage on his own.

The second he left, the wind began to howl and I felt sick with guilt. It was a long afternoon for me. The first thing he said when he returned home was, "Why didn't you drive me, Mommy? I was late. The wind pushed me back. I kept stopping and leaning against the trees."

I nearly died when I heard that. I wanted to gather him up in my arms and say, "Oh you poor baby! What a horrible mother you have."

But I didn't. I said, "Wow! What a walk you've had! All those long blocks in that bitter wind. That took endurance! That's the kind of thing you'd expect from Abe Lincoln, not a six-year-old boy!"

At that time I was delighted with myself because David seemed so proud. Looking back now, I got a new insight into what had taken place. Had I given him my guilt, he would have felt weak, sorry for himself, and in control of me. Instead, I gave him my admiration for his struggle, and that told him he was strong; that he could withstand hardship.

So much to think about. . . . So many unfamiliar concepts to mull over and make my own.

Chapter XII
Anger

1. A Beast Within

Dr. Ginott gestured toward the attractive young woman seated on his right. "Ladies," he said, "we have a guest this afternoon—Mrs. Bennett. She's a reporter for a national magazine and plans to write an article about us."

I thought, "How flattering! And how presumptuous! Look at her sitting there with that cool, superior expression. How could this complete stranger, someone totally unfamiliar with our approach, sit in on a single session and then report—probably in a few breezy paragraphs—on work that had taken us years to internalize! Well, this afternoon would be a revelation to her."

Every woman was a little brighter, a little sharper than usual. We tackled problems that would have stumped a Solomon. We even dredged up a few showcase stories from the past. We outdid ourselves.

When the session was over, Mrs. Bennett thanked us politely. "This has been most enjoyable," she said, "but I get the impression that coping with your anger is your greatest problem. Is that right?"

We were stunned. If after all she had heard, that was the only comment she could come up with, then obviously we hadn't even made a dent. Several women started to talk at once:

ROSLYN: I wouldn't say that! I mean, anger is a problem, but it's certainly not our biggest problem.

EVELYN: Of course I'm speaking only for myself, but I'd say that the area of sibling rivalry presented more difficulties to me.

Helen drew herself up in her seat and in her most elegant diction said, "Mrs. Bennett, our concern here is with a vast range of human emotions. Now obviously coping with one's anger is never simple, but it's a distortion to single out that particular emotion and label it our 'greatest problem.' Perhaps if you were to visit us again, you'd see that anger is just a small part of a much larger picture."

Mrs. Bennett wilted under the verbiage.

On the way home we marveled at her density. She hadn't understood at all. "Too young," we concluded. "Probably not even a parent." And we dismissed her from our minds.

The following week the phone rang as I was saying goodbye to the children. It was Helen. Her voice was strained. "Have they gone yet?"

"Why? What's the matter?" I asked.

"It all happened so fast," she said. "Billy was almost out the door when I noticed he was only wearing his sneakers. Now he's been sick in bed all week, and there's still slush and snow on the ground. I could feel my gorge rising, but I controlled myself. Very calmly I said, 'Billy, your boots.' He said, 'I don't need them; only babies wear boots.'

"Suddenly I found myself snarling at him. 'What is the matter with you? Are you stupid or are you deliberately trying to make yourself sick again? Just because some idiot fourth-grader decided that boots are out of style! Haven't you missed enough school this winter?'

"I threw the boots at his feet. He screamed, 'I hate you!' at the top of his lungs and I slapped him across the face. He shrieked, 'My ear! my ear!' And then I saw it—the imprint of my whole hand on his face and ear."

"Oh, no," I murmured. (My mind flashed back to that terrible incident last week between David and me. I had a strong urge to tell Helen about it, but something held me back.)

"Wait—there's more," she said. "Then he ran into the bathroom, saw himself in the mirror and cried, 'Look what you did to me! I'm going to show everyone in school what you did to me!' "

That was too much. I gritted my teeth and decided to tell her. "I did something to David recently that I'm not exactly proud of either."

"You hit him?" Helen asked hopefully.

"Worse," I said. "I called him 'the King of the Rats.' "

"I feel better already," Helen sighed. "At least I'm not the only one. What did David do to earn his title?"

"That's what's so strange. I don't even know what he did. It was what I *thought* he did. I heard Andy's voice from the bedroom pleading, 'David—STOP!' I started to dash in, then decided, no, I won't interfere, I'll let them work it out themselves. Then I heard Andy call out again, only this time it sounded as if he were being strangled. And on top of it all that big ox David was laughing gleefully. I went berserk. I charged into the room and grabbed him by the shirt collar. 'Do you know what you are?' I shouted. 'You're a rat. You're the King of the Rats! And do you know what? You're no son of mine. Because you must have a rat for a mother!' Then I pushed him away from me. He looked so little all of a sudden —so beaten. I've been sick about it ever since. I don't know why I said what I did. I only know that at the moment I couldn't stop myself. That was the most frightening part. It was as if there were two of me. One was spitting out all this venom, and the other was standing by watching—like some helpless imbecile."

For a while Helen was silent. Then in an incredulous voice she said, "Jan, do you realize what we've been saying? We've been saying that with all we know, we still aren't able to exercise self-control when we're angry. I slapped Billy in the face this morning and last week you practically disowned David. And for what? For not wearing boots? For teasing a brother? I don't know . . . I'm beginning to think that it doesn't really matter what we've learned in the group because there's a certain point at which it all gets canceled out. And *she* saw it."

"Who saw what?"

"That reporter. She picked it up immediately. That we couldn't handle our angry feelings. But we were too busy showing off to even consider her comment. If I met her today, I'd say, 'Mrs. Bennett, you're a very perceptive woman. We do indeed have a problem. We're all loving, stable, skillful parents until we get angry. Then, boom! All the layers of civilization are stripped away and we're right back to Neanderthal Man.' "

Gloomily, I pursued Helen's train of thought. "Why give us that much credit? Our responses probably go even farther back on the evolutionary scale. I read about an experiment once describing the reactions of rats and monkeys who had been provoked into anger. The scientists shocked them electrically, gave them occasional blows upon the head, and devised all sorts of ways to frustrate them."

"What happened?" asked Helen.

"The poor creatures turned on each other—biting, tearing, clawing—sometimes to the death. It seemed that when the animals were angry enough—frustrated enough—certain physiological changes took place that actually made it satisfying for them to hurt or destroy each other."

"Are you suggesting," Helen said, "that when our children make us angry that *we* behave like animals? That somehow we've got to attack them because it's physiologically satisfying? In that case, there's no hope for us!"

When the group met again, we confronted Dr. Ginott with our harrowing thoughts. He seemed interested but unperturbed. "It's true," he said, "when we're provoked, we do want to attack. But we're not monkeys or rats. We're human beings. And as human beings we have a choice. We can choose to find a human way—a civilized way—to express our savage feelings."

"That's not so easy," Helen said.

"To be human is never easy," answered Dr. Ginott. "It's always a struggle. And do you know when you can rest from that struggle? The day you die. We had all better be aware of what lurks within each of us. Protect me from the man who doesn't recognize his own potential for cruelty, lasciviousness, and bestiality."

Helen's face flushed. "I know *my* potential," she said. "I hit Billy last week."

"The way you put it!" Katherine laughed. "You make yourself out to be some kind of criminal. What's so terrible about a hand taken to the seat of the pants at the appropriate time? I've found it can work wonders."

"Katherine," said Dr. Ginott, "if you've found something that works for you—fine! I'm still looking for other answers. I'm only too aware that it's possible to spank a child into obedience. But I don't fool myself for a moment. I know that each time I spank him, I'm also teaching him, 'When you're angry—hit!' Unfortunately, I've never known of a child who was spanked into becoming a more loving human being."

"I don't think I made myself clear before, Dr. Ginott," said Helen. "I didn't just give Billy a little whack. We got into a big argument about his wearing boots, and it ended with my slapping him in the face. And the irony of it all is that two seconds before it happened, I said to myself, 'I am not going to make a big deal over anything as ridiculous as a pair of boots. I am going to control myself and speak calmly.' "

Dr. Ginott raised his eyebrows. "When have we ever said that a parent should speak calmly when he's boiling inside? The idea is not to hold back our anger, but to release it in short bursts, *before* it builds up into an explosion. Trying to be patient when you're angry is like applying the brake with one foot while the other foot presses the gas pedal. You wouldn't abuse your automobile that way. Be at least as good to yourself as you are to your car."

Evelyn smiled wryly. "I wonder if that's been my trouble—trying to be too patient. All I know is that when I finally do let loose, I. . . . Well, I don't hit, but I do say some pretty mean things. And I'm not so sure that my words don't hurt more than a spanking."

Dr. Ginott nodded. "Words can cut like knives. Some can even leave permanent scars. And that is why *anger without insult* remains our only civilized alternative to methods that dehumanize. And we still haven't got all the answers. The search to find new and more human ways to express the old and powerful emotion of anger is the work of a lifetime."

"In that case," said Helen, "I'd better get started right now. Dr. Ginott, would it be all right if we took time out today for some of the women to tell us what specific skills they use when they're angry. I think that might be helpful to me."

"I'll tell you what skill made a difference in my life," Nell said slowly. "I can still see Kenneth playing ball in the living room and me running after him, angrily explaining that the lamps were expensive, that I worked hard for my money, and that I expected by this time he would know enough to have respect for my possessions. Nothing I ever said made an impression upon him, so I thought perhaps I wasn't explaining myself very well. Then one day I heard Dr. Ginott say, '*Authority calls for brevity. Only the weak explain themselves.*'

That was an important day for me. The next time I caught Kenneth inside with the ball, I said very firmly, 'Kenneth, the rule is: Ball playing is to be done out of doors!' He must have been stunned by the change, because he just looked at me, gave the ball one more bounce, and went outside."

Helen listened with great interest. "I like that, she said, "getting rid of all the wishy-washy talk and boiling everything down to: 'The rule is. . . .' "

"Do you know what helped me, Helen," Roslyn said. "I used to threaten the children whenever they made me angry. Then at one of the sessions here, we talked about giving choices instead of threats. I went home and tried it, and I must admit it really makes a difference. For instance, if I ever see my kids playing ball in the house, I say, 'You have a choice. You can play with the ball outside or give up the privilege. You decide.' It doesn't work all the time, but it's better than telling them they're going to 'get it' when their father gets home."

Lee looked as if she could hardly wait for Roslyn to finish talking. "If you want to talk about anger, Helen, then I may be the person with the most experience," she said. "I've got a very short fuse. My husband says I yell first and think later. But I'm changing. I still yell because, well, that's me; but now instead of calling the kids names, I yell the thing I want them to remember.

"For instance, just after the last snowstorm, I saw my older boy throwing snowballs at my younger one, who, incidentally, was about to cry. My old way would have been to yell out the door, 'Cut that out, you big bully! Go pick on someone your own size!' This time I thought to myself, 'Hold it. I've got to convert all my anger into something useful. You know, like converting rushing water into electricity. Okay, so what is it I want them to know? And how do I say it in a short way so it'll stick in their heads?' Then when I finally had the sentence in my mind, I opened the door and yelled, 'Snowballs may be thrown only by mutual consent!'

"My big boy called back, 'What's mutual consent?'

" 'Something two people agree to,' I answered.

" 'Well I don't agree,' said the youngest.

" 'Okay, so we'll stop,' said the oldest. And that was that."

"That's an interesting conceptualization, Lee," said Dr. Ginott. "There's such a short time that a child lives at home and so much for him to learn before he goes out into the world. Wouldn't it be wonderful if parents could harness the energy generated by their anger and use it—not for insult—but for giving their children information and values."

We spent the rest of the session talking about other ways to express our anger helpfully. By the time we left I was numb. I was glad Helen was behind the wheel coping with the rush hour traffic. It gave me time to think. Helen had been so open and I hadn't spoken once. Why not? Because I was still too raw from my fight with David? Because everyone else sounded so sure of herself?

What had been eating at me all during that session? Was it fear? The fear that whispered, "It's no use. You're in a different category altogether. No skill on earth could have saved you from that exchange with David. The fury you felt toward him that morning wouldn't yield to the mere mouthing of words. Nothing could have controlled that poisonous eruption. There are some situations and some people for which nothing, *nothing* works!"

Control. . . . I tried to remember what Dr. Ginott had said about control. Had I tried too hard to control myself? Would it have made a difference if I hadn't held back that morning, but had instead run into the room at Andy's first outcry and shouted, "That makes me furious!"? And how about Helen? Would it have made a difference if she hadn't told herself to keep calm with Billy? Could the awful blowup really be avoided by the quick release of our angry feelings?

But the language of anger without insult didn't come quickly or easily to me. (The language of love, yes. I was never at a loss when it came to praise and endearments.) Could *that* be where the trouble lay? Was part of my anger caused, not only by what I was angry about, but also by my inability to express that anger? Could it be that if I had all the nonhurting words of anger at my command—all the subtleties of anger in my tongue—that my wrath would never build up to such a pitch again? That I'd never have to suffer the guilt and humiliation that comes from attacking my own child?

I took my first deep breath of the day. I told Helen that we had work to do tomorrow morning. Somehow we had to figure out, write down, and commit to memory fifty different ways to express the full gamut of our angry feelings. If we could just match the language of anger to the mood of the moment, we might be able to eliminate the horror of the explosion forever!

2. Matching the Message to the Mood

The next morning we were all business. We sat at the kitchen table with sharpened pencils and large yellow legal pads. Our goal was clear: to master the language of anger without insult.

What we needed was a situation guaranteed to raise parental ire. We settled upon "The Case of the Neglected Pet." Was there a parent anywhere who had ever bought a pet for a child who didn't find that after the first flurry of excitement of feeding the cat, walking the dog, or cleaning the fishtank, that the child's interest had waned and the parent, in addition to all his other chores, had become the animal's sole source of survival?

Only last week I had walked past the birdcage and seen the children's pet canary, George, sitting in a pile of moulting feathers, pecking frantically at an empty food dish. I was outraged. Through clenched teeth I told the children that they were cruel, rotten, and irresponsible; that they didn't deserve to have a pet; that maybe I'd skip *their* supper tonight so *they* could see how it felt to go hungry.

Now, in the calm of my kitchen, and without the distraction of the children, Helen and I would write down some other possibilities of what might have been said. (Almost anything would have been an improvement over the original.) Together we would note the gradations of our angry feelings, from mild irritation to extreme agitation, and match them to a language of "anger without insult." To give shape and order to our thoughts, we decided upon the following format. We would describe the parent's mood, the parent's message to himself, and then give examples of language that would express both the mood and the message. Here's what we wrote.

Let us suppose, at the beginning, that the parent (me, in this case) has been feeling good. She enters the room cheerfully and then spots the neglected canary. Her mood shifts—slightly.

MOOD: Mild Annoyance

INNER MESSAGE

Children are childlike. They need, and will continue to need, reminding for many years to come—often about the same things. Part of my job as parent is to guide and remind.

LANGUAGE

I. *The Gesture*

The gesture has immediate, dramatic impact. It also spares the parent the effort of speech.

a) I could have pointed meaningfully to the empty dish.

b) I could have unhooked the food dish from the cage and handed it to one of the children.

II. *The Note*

A note can be a powerful form of communication to a child, especially when signed "Love, Mother."

a) EMERGENCY! ! ! ! BIRD SIGHTED IN DIRE DISTRESS. WHO WILL SAVE HIM???

b) Riddle: Who is yellow, sings like a bird, and needs a square meal? Please solve and resolve.

c) (Less clever, but just as effective) GEORGE NEEDS TO BE FED! NOW!

III. *The Simple Descriptive Statement*
This belongs in the same category as "The milk spilled."
By describing, instead of commanding, I invite the child
to take responsibility.
a) "George looks hungry."
b) "George is pecking at an empty dish."

IV. *The Simple Descriptive Statement Repeated*
It's very tempting, after having had your first statement
ignored, to fly off into paragraphs of explanations and
accusations. But if my mood still holds and I have a well-
phrased statement, I'll trust it, hang on, and with quiet
deliberation, repeat:
a) "George looks hungry."
b) "George is pecking at an empty dish."

V. *Invitation to the Children to Work Out a Solution*
For long lasting results nothing beats involving the children in the problem-solving process. No matter what solution they come up with—and some of their ideas can be
pretty far out— there's at least a fighting chance of success
when it's *their* plan that *they've* drawn up *themselves.*
They have an inner commitment to see that it works.
(Even it if doesn't, they can always make revisions later
on.)
    "Children, something is bothering me. I need your
help. When George first came to this house he was fed
regularly. Now I notice that because of school and
practice pressures, he's often forced to skip his meals.
Do you think you could work out a feeding schedule
you can all agree upon and show it to me after supper?" (The key to success here lies in the magic phrase
"you can all agree upon.")

MOOD: Edgy

INNER MESSAGE

This is beginning to get to me, so I had better discharge some of my irritation constructively.

LANGUAGE

I. *A Strong Statement of My Feelings*

Here we can give the basic "I am angry," or we can enlarge and innovate.

  a) "I just passed by the birdcage and I was appalled at what I saw!"

  b) "I'm annoyed and disappointed. Certain children vowed they would take faithful care of their pets!"

  c) (This next statement might even increase their vocabulary.) "I'm distressed, dismayed, disgusted, and disgruntled!" (One could also add "disheartened" and "disconcerted," but that might be overdoing it.)

II. *A Strong Statement of My Values*

As long as I'm raising my voice, I may as well say something worth remembering.

  a) "Pets need care!"

  b) "When an animal depends upon us, we don't let him down!"

III. *A Strong Statement of My Expectations*

  a) "It is expected that in this family the children will take care of their pet's needs."

  b) "I'm confident that my children will do what's necessary to prevent their pet from suffering."

IV. *The Three-Word Exclamation*

The three-word exclamation allows the angry parent to be loud, sharp, and short. At the same time it tells the child that he can figure out what needs to be done.

a) "David, the bird!"

b) "Jill, the seed!"

c) "Andy, the dish!"

MOOD: Mean!

I want to jolt them out of their complacency, worry them a little.

INNER MESSAGE

I'd like to snarl, "If you kids don't feed that bird by the time I count three, I'll _____ _____ _____!" But I won't. (I know that a threat is in reality an irresistible challenge to the children to do that which has been forbidden, in order to find out if the parent means business. I refuse to fall into that trap. There are other ways to reach them.)

LANGUAGE

I. *The Choice*

"Children, the choice is yours. One: You can feed your bird now. Two: You can put up with an angry mother. Which shall it be?"

II. *The Alert*

"Children, you are lucky. You have at least three minutes to fill the bird's dish with seed before my mean feelings get the best of me."

III. *The Substitution of "As Soon As" for "If You Don't"*

"As soon as George is fed we can talk about watching

your favorite TV program. Until then I'm in no mood to grant favors."

MOOD: Rage!

The bird is still unfed after countless reminders. I want to punish, get back at, hurt. The empty dish has become a symbol of the school bag I tripped over yesterday, the bicycle I hauled out of the driveway the day before, and all the toys, shoes, and puzzle pieces I've ever picked up and put away because I got tired of asking them to do it.

INNER MESSAGE

I'm going to unleash my fury and still not do damage.

LANGUAGE

I. *The "When I" Statement*

The temptation when one is in a rage is to start a sentence with "You are _____" followed by a stream of invective. What can save me here is the pure technicality of beginning my sentence with "When I_____" followed by a description of what I see and what I feel. Let it rip!

a) "When I ask over and over again that a little bird be fed, and I'm still ignored, I become incensed! I'm taking care of the feeding now myself—and I'm furious at having to do your job!"

b) "When I see a helpless creature suffering from neglect, I feel outraged! I feel like smacking every one of you, and giving the bird away to someone who will take proper care of him. Now you had all better stay out of my way for a long time because I'm not responsible for what I might say or do!!"

This was as far as Helen and I could take our exercise. Was there a point beyond this? Short of throttling the child, we didn't know what it was.

We reread our papers and felt good about what we had written. The only question that remained was: What would happen in a real moment of anger? Could we, under fire, manage to come up with an honest statement that matched out mood and still did no damage?

We'd have to see.

3. When Words Have No Effect

I asked permission to start the session. First I described the events and feelings that led Helen and me to work out our self-imposed assignment, and then I read what we had written. When I finished reading, Dr. Ginott nodded. "Janet, if self-control was one of your goals, then it seems to me that you're heading in the right direction. The more ways we have to express our anger, the better chance we have of holding on to our self-control. It's when we try to bottle up our angry feelings that we run the danger of an explosion.

"But you've achieved more than that. You could almost say that you two have been doing the work of alchemists. You've taken the base, hurtful stuff of anger and transformed it into the pure gold of language that at its best is helpful, and at its worst does no damage. And what richness and variety I hear in the expression of your anger! You've shown that parents needn't be limited to such meager choices as name-calling and spanking."

"I don't mean to be picayune," Katherine said, "but it just seems to me that if this situation had been going on and on in my home, and I got down to that last stage of rage where I yelled that I felt like smashing the cage and giving the bird away, and the children still ignored me, I'd feel like a fool."

"And not without reason," said Dr. Ginott. "Certain situations should not be permitted to go 'on and on.' It's bad for the parent and bad for the child."

"I never thought about it that way before," Evelyn said. "But if it's true, then what can a parent do when words have no effect?

"I've talked myself hoarse to the boys sometimes—saying all the right things, too. I express my feelings; I describe the problem; I try to understand their feelings—but half the time they don't even bother to look up. It's like I'm talking to the walls. I don't know . . . sometimes I think I'm not in charge of my own children. It's more like they're in charge of me."

"And they will be in charge," answered Dr. Ginott, "unless they sense that you mean business. You know you are bigger than they are. You don't have to put up with unacceptable behavior. It would be a good thing for your children to know that behind your words lies the readiness to take action."

Evelyn seemed taken aback. "But Dr. Ginott," she protested, "I thought you were opposed to punishment."

"That's correct, Evelyn," he said. "I am. In a loving relationship punishment has no place. Can you imagine what would happen if your husband punished you for not having dinner ready on time? But I didn't say punishment; I said action. Unless a child knows that we are prepared to take action to protect our values and enforce our rules, our words are meaningless. If I were to say to a child, 'Ball playing in the house bothers me. You can play with it outside or put it away. You decide.' I had better be prepared to take the ball away if he continues. I could say as I remove the ball, 'Jimmy, I see you decided.'

"Have I made myself clear? Can you see that my intent was to halt his unacceptable behavior and still preserve his dignity? Notice I wasn't vengeful; I didn't question his character; I didn't even try to teach him a lesson. And yet, by taking the ball away, I demonstrated dramatically that I took myself seriously—that my feelings were not to be ignored."

Evelyn looked puzzled. "But how would that relate to Janet's problem? Suppose she really were getting upset about the bird? And suppose she really had tried all those things she wrote about, and nothing worked? What action could she take? About the only thing left to do would be to give the bird away —and that would be too cruel."

"Cruel to whom?" asked Dr. Ginott. "The cruelty I see here is to the parent who allows himself to be tormented every day by the same problem. Again, what's important is our attitude. We wouldn't say, 'Good, you got just what you deserved. Maybe now you'll learn!' No. Even in this drastic step of taking a child's pet away, we can still communicate in terms of our feelings and our values. 'Children,' we can say, 'I find myself getting too upset seeing a creature suffer in my home. When I'm faced with the choice of keeping our pet and being an angry mother or giving our pet away and being a pleasant mother—you know which I'll choose.' "

In obvious distress, Evelyn said, "Suppose they cry and carry on?"

"Did I ever give the idea that when we take action, children accept it graciously? Any child of spirit will protest and complain. And when he does, I can say, 'You wish we could have kept the canary. He brought much joy to our home. But he needs to be in a place where he can receive proper care.' "

Evelyn still fretted. "But suppose they ask for another chance?"

"Another chance!" Katherine burst out. "They've already had a thousand chances!"

"Children should have a thousand chances," said Dr. Ginott. "And you know what?" he smiled. "When they've used those up . . . they should have one chance more. We can say to the children, gently, 'Not now. Now is not a good time to talk about another canary. In a month or six weeks, bring up the subject again, and we'll all see how we feel about it then.' "

Evelyn thought awhile. "I can accept everything you say intellectually, but when I try to picture myself doing it, I realize I couldn't. I can just see the whole scene—my children hysterical and heartbroken, and me the bad one—the one responsible for making them unhappy. I couldn't stand it."

"Evelyn, *a parent's responsibility is not to his child's happiness; it's to his character.* By focusing only upon a child's happiness, we do him no favor. What kind of values would we be passing on to our children if we permitted cruelty to animals? Did you know that 'No' can be a loving response? Did you know that when we take action to stop a child's unacceptable behavior, we are doing him a service? What's more we are showing him how to be the kind of adult who can stand up for what he believes in."

I looked around the room. As Evelyn was agonizing, everyone was writing furiously. They couldn't get it down fast enough.

I didn't write. My head was spinning with new thoughts and old memories. Years ago, before I had children, I had stood transfixed, watching a woman and her son in Macy's. The mother snarled—her teeth bared.

"You're going to take that jacket whether you like it or not!"

The boy, pale and defiant: "I won't. You can't make me."
"Oh yes I can."
"I won't wear it!"
The woman's veins stood out on her neck. Her eyes narrowed to slits. "You're just asking for another punishment, aren't you? You haven't had enough, have you? All right, I'll take away your bicycle. Is that what you want? I guess it isn't enough that I've taken away your allowance and television!"

The moment was etched in my memory. The boy's face hard with hatred—his eyes flashing, "I'll get back at you." The mother, sputtering with rage—trapped in the web of her own words. She would either have to make good on every one of her threats or be a liar.

I had sworn to myself then and there that, when I had children, punishment would be no part of our relationship. I would never get sucked into that ugly vortex of crime and punishment—no matter how strong my itch to get even. Maybe that was why I hadn't been able to give the bird away! Even on paper. It would have seemed like a punishment to me.

But now Dr. Ginott was telling us about a way that parents could take strong action and still be on their child's side. We could take action, not in a punitive spirit, not to get back at our children, but to put a stop to behavior that had gone too far. We could be both forceful and caring at the same time.

I had found out something very important today—but I didn't know whether I could apply it. I wrote in my notebook: NOT PUNISHMENT—ACTION!

4. Action and the Limits of Action

I lay in wait for a chance to put "action" into action. The children were not at all cooperative. For the next few days they were unnaturally agreeable—even to each other. But they couldn't hold out indefinitely, and one afternoon opportunity knocked—in fact, it pounded.

David was making life miserable for Jill and Andy—teasing them to the point of tears. I made several attempts to appeal to his better nature, and when that failed I took action. It seemed to me to be just the right sort of action too. Not punitive but a kind of firm, restraining action.

I was so pleased with how I conducted myself that I was eager to tell the group all the details of what had transpired. But practically everyone had a hand raised at the beginning of the next session.

Helen suggested we take numbers, but Evelyn rose from her chair and demanded the floor first. Evelyn, whose every gesture was one of hesitancy—Evelyn, who had once sorrowfully described herself as a "marshmallow"—Evelyn, whose greatest fear was being too harsh, stood there and said, "I did it. I took action. I'm a tiger!"

We all laughed. "Tell us about it," said Dr. Ginott.

"It happened the day after our last meeting. I was in the shoe store with the twins and the store was crowded. Suddenly both boys decided to have a tug-of-war with the measuring stick. I put an end to that game and then they started chasing each other around the fitting stools. Normally I would have whispered, "I'm embarrassed," and prayed for the salesman to come quickly. Not this time. This time I caught each of them by the arm and said firmly, 'The people in this store are not to be disturbed! Now you boys have a choice. One: You can sit quietly. Two: We can leave. You decide.' They behaved themselves for about thirty seconds and then they started up again. I felt no hesitation inside of me. I got up, put on my coat, and said, 'I see you decided. Let's go.' And I walked out of the store. They ran after me, crying and tugging me back. 'But you said you'd buy us new sneakers.'

'That's right,' I answered, 'and I will—when you're ready to wait quietly.'

'We'll wait quietly now,' they said in chorus.

And then I borrowed your phrase, Dr. Ginott. I said, 'I'm not feeling emotionally hospitable now,' and started the car. How do you like that?"

"The important question," said Dr. Ginott, "is how did *you* like it?"

"I loved it," Evelyn said. "I felt so strong so . . . so in charge that even their crying didn't get to me. I didn't even mind having to make another trip to the shoe store at the end of the week."

Before anyone in the group could even comment on Evelyn's metamorphosis, Helen announced, "Another liberated woman will now give testimony. Evelyn, I was with you in spirit this week. In fact, I have my account in writing."

Then she read:

Friday morning, November 3. I open my eyes and nervously think, "Will Billy make the bus today or will I have to drive him to school again?" Though I wake up every morning with the same question on my mind, I already know the answer. The odds are that within the hour, I'll be sitting behind the wheel with a coat thrown over my nightgown, rollers in my hair, scared to death that I'll either run out of gas or be stopped by a policeman.

At the beginning of the term I thought that maybe there was something about the idea of going to school that was making Billy dawdle. But when we had a talk, everything seemed fine. He was happy with his teachers, his subjects, and had lots of friends.

Once I heard him out, I talked about my feelings. I told him how much I disliked being a combination alarm clock and chauffeur—and that I wished he would work out his own plan for making the bus on time.

For a few days after that he did make an effort; but then, little by little, I found myself back in the old routine again.

"Billy, it's 8:15. Your bus leaves at 8:30."

"Billy, it's 8:20 now and you're still in bare feet."

"Billy, would you like me to pack your schoolbag for you? You only have five minutes."

"Billy, I'm ready to climb the walls! It's 8:29 and you're still playing with baseball cards!"

"Billy, I'm furious! The bus just left. Get in the car."

Helen put down her paper for a moment. "At our last session, Dr. Ginott, you said that certain situations should not be permitted to go on and on because they're unhealthy for both the parent and the child. When I heard that, I said to myself, 'I've got one of those situations. Not only am I making myself crazy every morning, but Billy is being deprived of the natural consequences of being late. His punctuality had become *my* problem instead of *his*.

"But I still didn't see how Billy would get to school if I didn't drive him. You don't have to be an overprotective mother to notice that a mile is a long way for a little boy. And there are some dangerous intersections. I discussed the problem with my husband. Half jokingly he said, 'Maybe you ought to ship him off in a taxi the next time he pulls that nonsense. And make him pay for it out of his allowance.' Jack may have been kidding, but the idea appealed to me."

Helen picked up her paper and continued reading: That same evening I told Billy that having to drive him to school made me tense and irritable, and therefore I wouldn't be doing it anymore. If he were ever to miss the bus again, we could call a cab—and I'd even pay for it—the first time.

He listened but I don't think it penetrated because he just said, "Yeah, yeah, yeah," and left the room.

The next morning I woke up feeling as if a weight had been lifted from me. I watched 8:15, 8:20, and 8:29 go by and wasn't even tempted to tell Billy his time was running out. About 8:35 Billy finally looked up from his comic book and noticed the clock. He said, "Hey Mom, I missed the bus. You'll have to drive me."

Then I told him, "Billy, yesterday I said that from now on, in case the bus is missed we'll call a cab." I went to the telephone, and he tugged at my arm as I was dialing. "But I don't want to go alone in a taxi!"

"Mmmm, I can understand that," I said.

He continued to complain until the cab pulled up—but he did go. And since then he hasn't been late once! In fact, just the other morning he was hurrying *me* along. He said, "Haven't you got my lunch ready yet, Mom. I don't want to have to take that stupid taxi again."

Helen looked up from her paper, suddenly a little unsure. "Do you think that was too rough an action I took? Even if it *did* work? My sister thought it was mean of me."

"As I listened to you, Helen," said Dr. Ginott, "I said to myself, "Here's a mother who saw that she was in danger of becoming a doormat, and found the strength to do an about-face. She found a creative solution to protect both herself and her child."

I thought, "That's it, isn't it? Unless you take action, all the talk in the world just becomes a lot of blather. You *do* become a doormat—useful at times, but who listens to a doormat?" Aloud, I said, "I had an experience, too, where I found myself getting nowhere with words and was finally forced to take action. Only I had to perform in front of an audience—my next door neighbor.

"I was standing with her in the driveway exchanging pleasantries when Andy came rushing up with, 'David won't let me on the swings. He said Daddy bought them for him.' My neighbor eyed me sharply. Very calmly I replied, 'Tell David that Mommy said in our family the swings are to be shared by all.'

"I turned again to my neighbor. She went on in tedious detail about how her son had just been accepted at Yale. Then Jill appeared in tears. 'David pushed me!' she sobbed. My neighbor watched me intently. ('I hate her,' I thought. 'Her kid just got into Yale and mine can't get past swings.')

"I put an arm around Jill and said, 'You didn't like being pushed, did you? Tell David the rule is: No Pushing! If he's feeling angry, he can express himself in words.' Jill stopped crying for a moment, considered my comment, and ran back. No sooner had she left than Andy reappeared. This time *he* was crying. 'David punched me,' he wailed.

"I was incensed. Neighbor be damned! I didn't care what she thought. All the outrage I had ever felt at being the persecuted, youngest member of the family boiled up within me. I wanted to go back there and beat the bully until he begged for mercy. VENGEANCE!!!

"Well that's what I wanted to do, but what was that new thing I was going to try?—Something about taking action to stop obnoxious behavior without being vengeful about it. How would I do it in this case? How could I even think with that woman staring at me?

"I excused myself, walked back to the swings and said, 'David, in!' With my hand on his shoulder, I steered him toward the house.

"I didn't hit him *that* hard," David protested.

"In!"

"But that's not fair!"

"Who's talking about fair?" I answered. "I'm talking about my feelings. I feel strongly that you should be separated from your brother and sister until you can work out better ways to play with them."

"Wow!" Evelyn exclaimed approvingly. "You never once insulted David and yet you stuck to your guns. Maybe this is what we've all been looking for. It seems to work every time—for all of us."

"Not so fast," said Dr. Ginott. "While I go along with Jan's action, I'm always suspicious when we view any one particular skill as a cure-all. Human relations are seldom simplistic. Tell me, did everyone have such a positive experience? What became of all the other hands that were raised a while back? Let's not be intimidated by the success stories. We welcome your doubts too."

"Well, I hate to be the one to put a damper on things," said Roslyn. "But I think you'll have to admit that there are some situations where the children have you in a bind—where there just isn't any action you can take—and the kids end up getting away with murder."

A few women asked for an example.

"Well, just last Sunday the family was getting ready to visit my mother for dinner. I was hurrying everyone along because my mother gets very upset when we're late. She always has her dinner timed to the minute. Just as we were about to leave, my six-year-old decided to take off his shoes. And no amount of urging could convince him to put them back on. He wanted Mommy to do it. I wasn't quite dressed yet, so the other children tried—but he only kicked at them. And all the time my husband was sitting in the car honking the horn.

"Oh, I wanted to take action all right. I wanted to leave him home. But where was I going to find a baby sitter at two o'clock on a Sunday afternoon? So I ended up on my hands and knees putting shoes on a boy who ties his own shoes for school every day."

"Your point is well taken, Roslyn. In dealing with children we often come up against situations in which our options are limited. But if we go back to basic principles, we usually find that we're on solid ground. And one of our basic principles is being authentic with a child. Along with our services we can also give him our genuine displeasure. For example, 'Son, I don't like having to put on your shoes, but I'm doing it anyway. And now I'm displeased.' "

"But isn't that still giving in to him—still giving him a victory?" Roslyn asked.

"A child soon finds that a victory that comes at the cost of his parent's goodwill is a hollow victory," Dr. Ginott answered. "Mother's disapproval weighs heavily upon a child. It takes the flavor out of everything. Grandma could bake him his favorite cake, but to him it wouldn't taste so sweet."

There was a long, thoughtful silence. Then Evelyn spoke. "Well, maybe so," she said, "but if I were in that spot and gave one of my boys my so-called displeasure, the first thing out of his mouth would be, 'You don't love me!' "

Dr. Ginott frowned at an imaginary child. Sternly he intoned, "Now is not a good time to talk about love! *Now* is the time to put on shoes. Now is the time to make sure that Grandma is not kept waiting! Later in the car, we can talk about love."

"I get it," nodded Evelyn. "You don't let him distract you or make you feel guilty. You stick with the idea of doing what has to be done."

"If we're talking about how to handle ourselves in a tight situation," said Lee, "let me say that I'm a big believer in the teamwork approach. There's just so much I can do by myself and then I need a hand. Last night, for instance, Jason was banging on his drums while I was trying to get dinner ready. I asked him to hold off playing until after we had eaten because the sound was bothering me. Without missing a beat he said, 'Oh everything bothers you. You're getting old. Buy yourself earplugs.'

"I was ready to kill him. I asked myself, 'What action can I take? Remove the drums? They're too heavy. Remove Jason? He's too heavy. I didn't know what to do. At that moment my husband, bless him, stormed in from the bedroom, grabbed the drum sticks from Jason's hands and bellowed, 'I heard it and I didn't like it! Your mother said, 'After supper!' "

Dr. Ginott shook his head approvingly. "That's part of a father's job—to protect his wife from the abuse of the child. It's another way to tell our children that we don't sit back and permit the people we love to be assaulted—physically or verbally."

Another silence. Then Mary, a newcomer to our group, raised her hand. "I must be doing something wrong," she said. "I took action this week, but it didn't seem to work. Jody just turned four, and his grandparents bought him a magnificent fire engine for his birthday. He loves it so much I think he'd sleep in it if I let him. The only trouble is his room is slowly being wrecked. I don't mind the scratches, but I draw the line at holes in the wall. His idea of fun is to ring the bell, crash into the wall, and yell, 'FIRE!'

"Ordinarily I would have told him he was a bad boy and

punished him by taking away his fire engine. But this time I decided to try using some of the things I've learned here. So I told him, 'Jody, I don't like holes in the wall. You have an important choice to make. You can ride your fire engine and stay away from the walls or you can give up riding the fire engine in the house. Think about it for a while and let me know what you've decided to do.'

"Jody said immediately, 'I know now. I want to ride my fire engine. I'll be careful.'

"And he was careful—for about half an hour. 'It really works,' I thought. Then I felt the wall shake again. I was so mad, I said to myself, 'Once and for all this child is going to learn! It's time to take action.' I went into his room and hauled him out of his seat, kicking and screaming. Then I wheeled the engine into my room and locked the door. When he calmed down a little later, he said accusingly, 'You took my engine away. It's not yours. It's mine.'

"Very quietly I said, 'I don't like holes in my walls.' Now there wasn't anything punitive in the way I handled him. I took only the action that I thought would stop him. But that evening when I gave him back his fire engine, he started all over again. I don't know what to do now."

"Mary," sighed Dr. Ginott, "if we knew the kind of actions that would help a child learn 'once and for all,' we would type up a list, publish it, and send it to parents all over the world. But we don't. When a parent says to himself, 'Once and for all I'm going to end this child's unacceptable behavior,' he's already defeated. Children don't learn in terms of 'once and for all.' They learn in terms of 'now and then again, and still again.'

"But don't think your action wasn't helpful. It was. And you can try other ways. Perhaps you could give him in fantasy what you can't give him in reality. You could say, 'Jody, I bet you wish you lived in a house with padded walls so you could go bump with your fire engine any time you like.'

"And if that gets no results, maybe a road sign tacked up in his room that says REDUCE SPEED—WALL AHEAD will reach him." Dr. Ginott grinned. "Look, he'll be four words up on the other kids when he gets to kindergarten. But better still, you can present Jody with the problem and ask him what ideas *he* can come up with. And if none of these suggestions work, it might be best to limit the use of the fire engine to the sidewalk.

"The point I'm making is that action is not the 'final' solution. It's a temporary measure—only one of the many tools in our workshop. Valuable, yes; but not to be used without discrimination. A carpenter doesn't use a sledgehammer on a tack when the pressure of his own thumb will do the job.

"You notice, Mary, that my focus is not on obedience, but on *the process* of engaging a child's cooperation. It would be no great trick to keep Jody away from the walls. You could beat him, insult him, punish him and he'd never touch your walls. But what would happen to Jody inside? He'd hate himself, wish you dead, and on top of it all, feel guilty for wishing it. That's why my constant concern is the search for humane alternatives."

"I think I understand what you're talking about," Katherine said, her voice solemn. "In fact I might even be starting to live it. Something happened to me at our last session. Everything I heard that day suddenly connected and clicked together in my mind—Jan and Helen's report on anger, your comments about the difference between punishment and action. I think it may have made a permanent change in my relationship with Diane.

"I know I haven't spoken much about her. You've heard me talk mostly about the younger children. And there's a reason for it. I've felt that what I've learned here just didn't pertain to Diane. She's so defiant, so rebellious. 'No' has no meaning for her. She makes her own rules. Even my simplest, most reasonable request gets a nasty response.

"Recently, and I suppose it's because she's almost a teenager, she's been more impossible than ever. She pushes me so hard that in the end I have no choice except to punish her. Nothing else makes a dent. And even punishment would only stop her temporarily. I've never felt good about it. It was against everything you were teaching, but my husband is from the old school and has no patience with me when I try some of the ways I've learned here. He says I let her get away with too much. But I don't. I've punished her more times than I care to remember. And it was only because I never clearly saw any other alternative.

"But at the last session I got a whole sense of another way, and I just knew that somehow I would be different.

"That same night, Diane pulled one of her typical stunts. She had been skating in the park all afternoon and walked in at seven o'clock, full of excuses. (It was the third time in two weeks.) It's a good thing her father wasn't home. He might have taken a strap to her.

"Oh how I wanted to fix her. I wanted to cut off all her phone calls and forbid her to see any of her friends for a month! And then the picture of that whole cycle came to me: Diane does something wrong. I punish her. She does something worse to get back at me. I punish harder. She pays me back—in spades. And on and on and on!

"It took everything I had not to fall back into that old pattern again. 'I've been crazy with worry!' I yelled. 'Do you know what could happen to a young girl in the park at night? For two hours I've been pacing up and down this room. I was just getting ready to call the police!'

"She started making excuses, but I stopped her. 'If I listen to a single excuse now, it will only make me angrier. Maybe in

the morning. Anyway, I'm glad you're home. Now goodnight!'
And I left the room. . . . "That may not sound like much to
you, but it was a big change for me.

"A half hour later she breezed in as if nothing had happened.
Very cheerfully she said, 'Mom, I need new hair rollers. The
drugstore is still open. Can you drive me?'

"For a moment I considered her request. Then I shook my
head.

" 'Oh mother!' she said scornfully. 'Because of tonight?
That's ridiculous. Nobody attacked me, did they? The trouble
with you is you make such a big deal out of everything.'

"Very quietly I said, 'The park is not a safe place at night.'

"Her whole expression changed. 'So you're punishing me,
right? I suppose you won't let Daddy take me to the store
either.'

" 'What your father does is up to him,' I answered. 'If he
wants to take you, I won't stop him. . . . I can't. I'm still too
angry.'

"She tested me further. 'I bet you won't let me have a
friend over tomorrow, will you?'

" 'One thing has nothing to do with the other,' I said. And
I meant it.

"There were other incidents too—and with each occurrence,
something seemed to shift. There was a slight thaw, a relaxa-
tion of hostilities. Then one day the oddest thing happened.
She borrowed my sunglasses and lost them. When I expressed
my irritation, she stood there defiantly and said, 'Well, aren't
you going to punish me? What are you going to do to me?' It
was almost as if she were begging me to go back to the old
way. For the moment I didn't know what to say. My words
came slowly. 'Diane, it would seem to me that what's important is not punishment, but that you understand how I feel.
And it's also very important that I understand how *you* feel. I

feel very annoyed about my sunglasses being lost, and I think maybe you wish you were returning them to me right now.'

"She flashed me a look that was so . . . I suppose the best way to describe it was 'friendly.' I don't know what's going to happen from here on, but I do know that I never want to go back to the old way again."

"Katherine," said Dr. Ginott, "you have my deepest respect for your struggle. It seems to me that you're putting to use many of the principles we talk about here—and with a child who has not been easy.

"You've experienced for yourself the difference between the dead end of punishment and the open-endedness of a relationship built upon regard for each other's feelings."

He turned to the group. "You see when we punish a child, we divert him from facing himself. There are people who say, 'But if you don't punish him, you're letting him get away with murder.' Just the opposite is true. When we punish a child, we make it too easy for him. He feels he's paid for his crime and served his sentence. Now he's free to repeat his misbehavior.

"Actually, what do we want from a child who has transgressed? We want him to look into himself, experience some discomfort, do his emotional homework, begin to assume some responsibility for his own life."

Katherine listened and nodded eagerly. "And there's one more thing I'd like to mention. I think when a parent stops punishing, there's a side benefit for him too. For the first time in years, I find that I'm not feeling so guilty about Diane. I used to buy her extra clothes or take her places when I really didn't want to—just to make up for being so hard on her. Now I feel much more free to say no, and I find I can even say it without giving her an explanation."

There was another long silence. "I . . . I'm reluctant to say this," Nell said, almost inaudibly. "Everyone's been doing so well . . . I'm really a discordant note here . . . but I must confess I had a failure. What I mean is—I took action—I really did—but then I weakened when I should have held my ground." We all turned toward Nell respectfully. We knew what an effort it was for her to speak.

She continued, "I've been so annoyed about the abuse of the TV set that I decided to limit Kenneth's viewing to one hour a day. I think even that's too much, but Kenneth feels deprived. He always manages to squeeze in another fifteen or twenty minutes—and that galls me. I've scolded him about it a number of times, but when I walked in the other day and found that he had been sitting in front of the set for almost three hours, I decided that the time for talk was over. This had gone too far. The one-hour TV rule was going to be strictly enforced from now on.

"I was ready for him the following night. I timed him to the minute. When the hour was up, I walked into the room and snapped off the set.

" 'TV is finished for tonight, Kenneth.'

" 'But Mom . . . '

"I repeated, 'TV is finished for tonight.'

" 'But, Mom,' he said plaintively, 'there's a Special on whales tonight.'

" 'Oh, dear,' I thought, 'on this of all nights! He'd love watching a program on whales, and I'd love watching it with him. But I've got to hold firm.'

"I looked at his upturned face and didn't know what to do. Then I heard myself saying, 'Kenneth, I haven't forgotten what happened yesterday . . . I've decided to allow you to watch tonight!'—And do you know what he did? He took my hand and kissed it."

"Tell me, Nell," asked Dr. Ginott, "why do you feel you had a failure?"

"Well, I knew I was being inconsistent. I suppose Kenneth has already gotten the idea that his mother is a weakling, and thinks he can take advantage of me next time."

"With children, I never worry about next time. *We're* the ones who determine what a child can or cannot get away with next time. . . . In my eyes, Nell, you didn't have a failure. You felt that the need for sharing a beautiful moment with your son was more important than the need to be consistent. You trusted your inner voice, and when we heed that voice instead of sticking to the rigid rule, we usually don't go too far wrong. There is seldom a time we cannot demonstrate our humanity by saying, 'I've had second thoughts . . . ' 'I've reconsidered . . .' or 'Tonight we'll make an exception to the rule.' "

I listened and thought, "I'm privileged. I'm in rare company: Dr. Ginott with his unwavering insistence upon the ways that humanize, these women with their determination not to *go* backwards—women who at their most embattled moments stubbornly refuse to hit, punish, threaten, or insult."

Nothing I heard today sounded typical or even familiar. At no time did any of the women act vengefully. ("You're crying because you didn't get your sneakers? Good! I'm glad. Maybe now you've learned your lesson!")

At no time did they relate in terms of 'tit for tat.' ("You think it's all right to hit your brother, David? Well now *you're* going to get hit.")

At no time were they phony. ("Jody, taking away your fire engine hurts me more than it hurts you.")

At no time did they turn a child's offense into a character deficiency. ("So you've lost my sun glasses? That doesn't surprise me. You've always been careless.")

At no time were their responses excessive. ("You've brought it on yourself, Diane. For being late again, no ice-skating for a month.")

At no time were their responses irrelevant. ("For missing the school bus, Billy, you'll do without your allowance.")

Instead of any of these hurtful old cliches, I heard language that was nondamaging, honest, and skillful—language that dealt only with the specific incident at the specific moment.

I heard about the kind of action that halted unacceptable behavior and at the same time opened up the possibility that a child might look within. Change. Grow.

Suddenly I wanted very much to go home to my family.

5. And Still We Explode

I knew so much and I was glad for everything I knew. Hardly a day went by that I wouldn't have drowned in the emotional rapids of family life, had I not my skills to hang on to.

Take a typical morning. I awaken to the friendly buzz of Ted's electric shaver mingling with the innocent voices of the children chattering with each other. "I'm a lucky woman," I think. "Loving husband . . . beautiful kids."

Sleepily I step into the kitchen and don't even flinch at the sound of cornflakes crunching under my slippers. Why make an issue? With a pleasant "Good morning," I hand David the broom, Jill the dustpan, and pour Ted's juice. Even the sight of jellied fingerprints on the table doesn't throw me. "Quick Watson, remove the evidence before Daddy comes in!" I say, tossing Andy a sponge. The banter flies thick and fast as they clean up, and I think, "What a mother! What children! What a delightful family we are! It's a pity no one's watching us!"

And then the first poke—the first shove—the first name called—and all at once the children seem a little less adorable.

A second later a fight to the death for the last banana—the horror of watching its insides oozing out—Ted's juice splashing across the table as the elbow of the victor knocks his glass over.

Suddenly I find myself smack in the middle of another scene with an entirely different set of characters. In fifteen seconds flat, I've been cast in the role of besieged mother, with an irritable husband in the wings about to enter, grumbling about a juiceless breakfast. And the children! These disgusting children are nothing but a bunch of savages. The mood that made the moment before so lively and loving has vanished completely. (I can't even remember it.) In it's place comes a primitive longing to ATTACK! My spontaneous urge is to knock all their heads together—but I know where spontaneity will get me.

Now is the moment of truth. With goodwill gone I have nothing to go on but my skills. And there are many to choose from: I can describe the problem; help the children work out their own solution; state a rule; declare my expectations; assert my values; shout my indignation; write a note; give choices; take action; etc. I am rich with possibilities.

And I am effective.

It is almost too good to be true.

A suspicion grows in me. Maybe if I could just keep it up, I'd never be at the mercy of that tyrannical emotion again— never find myself reduced to a screaming, hysterical, attacking, lunatic again. I'd have anger licked. I'd be free at last!

Warily I watched the days come and go without serious incident. No matter what came up, I coped. At our next meeting other women reported that their new skills had dramatically reduced hostilities in their homes too. "We've got the answer," I thought triumphantly. "Pasteur discovered the anthrax vaccine, Salk eliminated polio, and we've found the formula for eradicating the family explosion."

I permitted myself a momentary fantasy. There I was in Sweden, stepping up to the podium to receive—on behalf of the group—the first Nobel Peace Prize for wiping out violence in the family. With missionary zeal I would announce to a distinguished audience that the formula was difficult, a little complicated, but not impossible. It could be learned and used by parents all over the world. Who knows what the implications might be for world peace? Cheers . . . Wild applause!

Reality came hard after that. I watched with dismay as, one by one, we fell from our state of grace—each at a different time—each for a different reason. There seemed to be certain events that temporarily overwhelmed us all—certain situations that pushed us beyond the limits of our skills, past the brink of our endurance, over the border of sanity and into the kind of behavior where we violated everything we believed in and were working toward.

In the car on the way into the city, Helen told me about her ordeal. Grimly she mumbled something about not knowing why she was even bothering to go to a meeting since she wasn't capable of applying anything she learned anyway. Then reluctantly she spoke of the painful events of her morning. She said that for a long time she had felt a growing concern about her husband's late hours and constant fatigue. This morning he seemed so tired that she found herself urging him to change his job. Jack didn't take kindly to her advice. He slammed down his coffee cup, shouted, "Dammit, you're a nag! Quit running my life!" and left—his breakfast unfinished on the table.

She was still reeling from the blast when Billy came into the kitchen and opened up the sandwich she had just made for him. "Yucchh!" he said in disgust. "Stinky old baloney again! You never make me anything good. All the other mothers make good things for their children."

Helen said that something snapped inside of her. "Don't

you tell me about the other mothers," she hissed. "If you're not satisfied with me, then get yourself another mother. Not that anyone would want you. And I don't care if you eat or not. It might do you good to go hungry!"

Billy flung his sandwich on the floor, kicked open the door, and ran crying to school.

Helen said afterwards, she sat there alone in the kitchen, staring at the bread and baloney on the floor, hearing her own voice over and over again: "Not that anyone would want you" . . . "Don't care if you eat or not." And Jack's voice, "Quit running my life." She said she felt like a nagging wife, a rotten mother—a total failure.

And at another time, Katherine, who had been so pleased with the way things were going between her and Diane, seemed stricken when she told us what happened.

She said that for the last few weeks, Diane had complained bitterly about her "mean" French and math teachers who "hated" her. Katherine listened sympathetically for a while and then ventured that it was probably all just her imagination. Why would anyone hate her? But inside there was the old clutch of anxiety. Was Diane becoming difficult again? Was this the beginning of a new problem? Maybe the work really was too hard for her.

Then the warning notes began to arrive from school. Diane was "unprepared for class" . . . "not paying attention" . . . "refuses to apply herself."

Katherine promptly called the school and met with both teachers. They assured her that her daughter was a bright girl, more than capable of doing the work. Feeling a little better, Katherine went home and told Diane that she had been mistaken all along. Actually her teachers thought quite highly of her. And now wouldn't she please try harder.

A month later the report card arrived. Not only was Diane failing math and French, but a new complaint had been added. "Continually disrupts class."

Katherine was furious. "To hell with the whole approach," she said to herself. "I've been tying myself down to the words I ought to say for too long. Now I'm going to let her have it—straight." She told Diane that she was an ungrateful brat taking advantage of two teachers who were doing their best to help her. She said she had felt ashamed to go to school and say whose mother she was. She said she was finished with her and that she'd have to sink or swim on her own now. Diane stared at her coldly and left the room.

Incensed, Katherine followed, shouting after her. "And don't think you can just turn your back on me! You'll be sorry this ever happened. Don't think for a minute that I'm not going to tell your father about this. And don't expect to have any friends over for the next month either!"

Katherine said that for the moment she felt justified in her attack. Diane had brought it upon herself, hadn't she? Well, maybe a little plain talk would knock some sense into her.

And then came the overwhelming pangs of contrition. "What have I done? In thirty seconds I opened my mouth and undid months of painstaking effort at rebuilding a relationship."

As for me, I listened to both women with a combination of compassion and clinical interest. I was sorry they had suffered, but it was easy to see what had brought it about.

It seemed that there were specific contributing factors that led to each explosion. The first was anxiety. An incident or a series of incidents occurs and suddenly the parent is gripped with fear. It's hard to be skillful when you're frightened out of your wits.

It was Katherine's anxiety that threw her off course. It was her fear that her daughter was on her way to developing a pattern of school failure that led Katherine to ignore her skills. The final explosion was almost inevitable. At no point along the way did she acknowledge Diane's feelings, and then she compounded the problem by suggesting that Diane try harder —a vote of no confidence, if ever there was one. Not much chance of change with that kind of approach.

The second factor that could set off an explosion was often unrelated to the child, except in a minor way. An outside tension could trigger an outsized reaction. It was Helen's run-in with Jack that made her attack her son. Under ordinary circumstances she could easily have handled Billy's complaint. I could just hear her saying, "Hey, I don't appreciate being compared to other mothers. If you have a complaint to make about sandwiches, then stick to the subject of sandwiches!"

Somehow I felt strangely invincible. It seemed to me that even under pressures such as these, anxiety, or outside tensions, I would have known what to do. But I hadn't bargained for yet a third category of trouble: the almost crazed reaction to the problem that persists and persists and never gets solved. For Lee it was, "He's lost his bite plate *again.*" For Mary it was, "He's run out into the street *again.*" In my case it was, "He's hurt his brother *again.*"

I saw David fling a pair of scissors at Andy that narrowly missed his eye, and I went temporarily insane. I tore into David and hit him wherever my hand could reach. Then I threw him onto his bed and screamed at him. "What are you trying to do? Kill your brother? Put his eye out? No one is safe when you're around. You're a monster!" Suddenly I felt a sharp pain in my thumb. It was swollen and blue. I must have broken a blood vessel hitting him the way I did.

I walked out of his room and stood there frozen. "What's the matter with me?" I thought. "How could I have behaved like that? I'm less than human. Maybe David will forgive me, but how can I ever forgive myself? And what a hypocrite I am! I'm all ready to change the world and I can't even change myself."

So there we were, all of us, back in the same old hole again: the attack, the remorse, the guilt. In complete despair, I thought to myself, "It's all been for nothing. It's been a huge waste—a waste of time and energy. I had been running and running, kidding myself into thinking I was making progress, only to find I had come full circle—back with those anger-crazed monkeys and rats again.

And what lengths I had gone to, to get away from them! Writing reports about neglected pets, watching the words out of my mouth, analyzing my feelings, examining my actions, analyzing everybody else's reactions. The whole thing was a little bit creepy.

But worse than any of these thoughts was my fear. I feared I had done irreparable harm to my child's self-esteem; I feared that David could never really trust me again; and though I wanted more than anything else to get back to our old relationship again, I feared that I wouldn't know how.

A part of me wanted to rush into David's room and beg his forgiveness, and another part wanted to drum it into his head how dangerous it was to throw sharp objects. I knew that either idea would only make matters worse, so I did nothing. Instead I took a long walk to the mailbox. And I didn't even have a letter to mail.

6. The Road Back

As I walked, I had an inner dialogue.

"Why had it happened?"

"Because brothers fight."

"But why is David always the aggressor?"

"He's jealous. He looked so resentful yesterday when he walked into the room and found me hugging Andy. Could that be why he went after him with the scissors?"

"Maybe it's simpler than that. Maybe Andy provoked him. Andy can be annoying at times."

"But David should be able to cope with it better."

"Why?"

"Because he's bigger and older."

"There you go again, still identifying with the baby of the family. Think for a while. Put yourself in his shoes. How would it feel to be the oldest? How would you feel if you were constantly pestered by a younger brother and your mother always expected you to go easy on him?"

"Sorry for myself . . . angry at my mother . . . bitter towards my brother. I'd want to hurt him."

"Suppose you finally did hurt him and your mother caught you? Suppose she called you a monster and beat you?"

"Okay, I get the point. But what do I do now? What *can* I do?"

"What do you mean, 'What can *you* do?' How about David? What responsibility does *he* bear? *He* threw the scissors. He's the one who has to face up to the consequences of that action. And *you're* the one to see to it that he does."

I felt my strength returning. I could go back to my son now.

I didn't know exactly what I'd say, but that didn't matter. My direction was clear: I would listen to David carefully. Then I'd state my own values, firmly—fiercely, if necessary. But there'd be no insult, and no groveling apology.

Back home from my walk, I knocked on David's door. No answer. I pushed it open and saw David lying face down on the bed. I sat down beside him. "Can you listen now, David?"

He made a small sound.

"I think what happened today hurt you very much—inside as well as outside."

"You didn't have to hit me," he mumbled into his pillow. "You could have just told me."

"That would have been a better way."

"So why did you?"

"I think you know, David. I think you know that what happened pushed me beyond my limit."

"Well Andy pushes me beyond *my* limit."

"You feel that he goes too far—that sometimes he pesters and pesters you until he really enrages you."

"That's right! He does! So what am I supposed to do? Stand there like a dummy while that nosey kid snoops around my drawers?"

"That can be pretty infuriating, your kid brother rummaging around in your drawers."

"You're not kidding! You always ask me to tell him in words how mad I get. But that doesn't always work. The only thing that will stop that creep is a fist down his throat."

"David, that's where we disagree. I can understand your stopping Andy—even with your hands if necessary—but violence? A fist down his throat? Throwing scissors? Oh, no!" I got up from the bed and stood over him. "In our home hurting is out. Strictly forbidden! NO CHILD MAY HARM ANOTHER CHILD!"

David hid his face in the pillow again. "You don't love me," he murmured.

I was unrelenting. "I care about you! I care about the kind of person you are! I expect you to work out your differences with your brother nonviolently. And if you ever find yourself running out of ideas for peaceful solutions, come tell me or Daddy and we'll see to it that you get help."

David rolled over on his back and stared at me. "That's no good. You always take Andy's side. You like him better."

"Is that how it seems to you?"

"That's not how it seems. That's how it is."

I thought a long time. Then slowly I said, "I'll tell you how it seems to me. To me it seems that each of my children is different and absolutely irreplaceable. I guess that's why I love each one, not equally, but differently. For instance, who else in the whole world looks like my son David, has his smile, his thoughts, his feelings—or his freckles?"

David looked pleased, but tried not to show it. Scornfully he asked, "Who likes freckles?"

"I do. Because they're part of you."

That was all. It was over. And it felt good to be David's sane mother once more.

Helen's attempt to get back to a better relationship bore some resemblance to mine. After the initial remorse, her great concern was whether or not she could put the pieces back together again.

Apparently it had meant a lot to her to be able to unburden herself in the car that day without having me evaluate her or tell her what to do.

She said that when she got home that afternoon, her impulse was to call Jack immediately and smooth things over, but then she decided against it. There had been enough talk, she thought. What Jack really needed was to have some of the pressure taken off. Tonight *she* would help the children with their homework. Tonight *she* would get the children off to bed.

Having thought that through, she called Billy into her room. He entered sullenly.

"Billy, I've been thinking a lot about what happened this morning. We were very angry with each other, weren't we?"

"You yelled at me," Billy said.

"Yes, I know. But I think maybe we both learned something. I found out that my son doesn't like baloney sandwiches, and you found out that your mother blows her top when she's spoken to in a certain way."

"What did I say that was so bad?"

"Billy, when you want something from someone, it's a good idea not to attack them; it's a good idea to ask in a way that makes it possible for the other person to listen."

Billy wasn't convinced. "So what am I supposed to say to you? 'Please dear mother, I kiss your feet. Please don't give me any more baloney sandwiches, your royal majesty.' "

Helen smiled. "That's one possibility. Another is 'Mom, would it be too much trouble to make something beside baloney sandwiches. I'm getting tired of them.' When I'm spoken to that way, Billy, it makes me feel like being helpful."

Billy chewed thoughtfully at a loose hangnail. "Well, I don't want to always say what you want me to say."

"I see," Helen said, momentarily thrown. "Then you may want to consider writing a note with specific suggestions."

"No," he said, "notes are stupid. I gotta go now, Mom. Jimmy's waiting for me."

"Well," Helen thought, "I really laid an egg with that one. But at least we're on speaking terms again. And maybe next time he'll give a little thought to how he asks for something he wants."

The next morning she was amazed to find an old piece of cardboard on her desk with a week's menu on it. It read:

> *Monday—tunafish*
> *Tuesday—jelly*
> *Wednesday—tunafish*
> *Thursday—jelly*
> *Friday—baloney, but only if there's no tunafish*

The following week Katherine described her reaction to her blowup with Diane. She said that for hours she had been too upset to function normally. She kept thinking, "I've made myself the enemy again. With all I've learned and with all I know, I've pushed us both right back into that old, dead-end, punishment routine. Now Diane can give up completely and blame everything on her 'cruel mother.' And she'd be right. Only it's not because I'm cruel. Just dumb.

"Why am I accusing myself? So I wasn't the perfect mother giving the perfect response. Doesn't a child bear some responsibility for his actions? I'm not the one disrupting classes. Diane is. . . . What would Dr. Ginott say? I suppose he'd say punishment wasn't what she needed. I guess he'd say she needed a parent who could be there *with her*—not *against her*—while she struggles toward her own solutions! . . . I don't know if I can do that. I don't know if I have the skill or the strength."

Little by little Katherine began to think about all of Diane's complaints about school. Maybe her negative feelings shouldn't have been denied. If she felt her teachers hated her, there probably was something to it. And even if there wasn't, her feelings still needed to be heard out.

But how about the other side of it? Diane was failing two subjects and using her "mean teachers" as an excuse to goof off. It would have to be made very clear that this was not an acceptable way to deal with the problem.

Then Katherine remembered that the school ran a tutoring program at a minimal fee. A neighbor's child had used the service with excellent results. That might be just the answer for Diane; a friendly high school student with whom she could be at ease, a purposeful youngster who could even be an inspiration to her.

Katherine began to feel better.

In her mind she formulated a rough draft of the areas she wanted to cover. First, she'd express her honest feelings, only this time she'd leave out the insults.

"When I saw that report card, I was so shocked, so disappointed, and so mad that I just boiled over. I said some things I didn't even mean. But I'm done with that now."

Second, she'd give Diane plenty of time to air whatever was on her mind. Consciously she'd listen to and reflect Diane's feelings.

"It's not easy to learn from teachers whom you feel don't like you—particularly with subjects as difficult as French and math."

She'd try hard not to get in the way of anything else Diane wanted to bring up. There might very well be other factors that would be uncovered with open-minded listening.

Third, she would work with Diane on finding solutions to the problem.

"Diane, these subjects have to be passed. Now *how* you go about passing them is up to you."

Perhaps they could explore the possibilities together. Perhaps a few suggestions at the right time would help.

"How do you think you'd feel about seeing your guidance counselor?" Or,

"You may want to consider using the tutoring service at school."

Katherine said she began to see more clearly what her role was. It was to give her child support while she tried to find some answers for herself.

When she finally did talk to Diane, she said that her actual words didn't come out nearly as smoothly as the ones she had rehearsed in her mind, but that the general ideas were the same. Diane didn't have much to say until the subject of the tutor came up. Then she shook her head.

"I don't need a tutor, Mom," she said. "There's a girl in my class who takes great notes. She can help me get caught up and it won't cost anything."

Katherine said that for the moment she was tempted to argue—to press for the tutor—but she held her tongue. Instead she said, "So you plan to take care of it yourself. I see." Then impulsively she put her arm around her daughter.

I had been chewing on the subject of anger for a long time. Like an old bulldog I had been gnawing on the same bone for months—sniffing every inch of it—turning it again and again —splintering the hard edges to get at the last bit of marrow.

Now I could lay it to rest. Somehow our three experiences, coming together as they did—Katherine's, Helen's, and my own—told me what I had been so driven to find out: *I didn't have to be so frightened of my anger. No one would be destroyed by it. Even if I lost all control—all was not lost. There would be a way back.*

What a relief! I'd no longer have to run the treadmill between guilt and despair. I could get off—move on. I had ways to help myself.

A whole new set of internal messages were stirring inside me. After the next explosion, I'd try to remember to say to myself:

"It's not the end of the world. Anyone can violate his own standards of behavior—given enough provocation. Don't be so hard on yourself. No more orgies of self-condemnation. Some of the guilt you can use—to prod yourself into making changes. The rest, push away or it will drag you down—paralyze you."

I'll say to myself: "My temporary breakdown doesn't define me. It doesn't tell me who I am. I am what I will choose to be —and I'm not finished yet. I'm still in the process of becoming. What happened was upsetting—regrettable—but much more important is how I will conduct myself afterwards."

I'll say to myself: "Don't panic if you can't figure out how to make repairs immediately. Allow yourself time—time to be alone with all your miserable feelings. Time for *not* having the answers. Time for living with uncertainty. There are no shortcuts. Only after you give yourself time, can you even begin to think in terms of being helpful again. And that will take as long as it has to take."

Then, when the painful, confused emotions have subsided a little, I'll try to think constructively. I'll ask myself whether something can be salvaged from the whole mess. Is there a new insight buried in the wreckage that I can ferret out and use for the future? Are there changes *I* have to make? Are there changes *my child* has to make? Can I find what I'm looking for by myself, or do I need the help of another voice, another ear?

And if I do find a useful truth, I'll think about how to state it simply, briefly, without blaming or moralizing. I'll use the language of empathy, language that describes, language that points a new direction, language that heals.

My feeling of calm was so total that it was hard for me to believe that I had once been so agitated. What had I been so afraid of? Why couldn't I have been more casual all along? I had often heard people say, "So I lost my temper. So I hit him and told him he was stupid. So what. He knows I don't mean it. Anyway it cleared the air. Once it's over, it's forgotten. No big deal."

But it *was* a big deal. There had been reason for my fear. The harm done by unbridled rage was never small. I had seen for myself how a series of explosions could chip away at even the best relationship, leaving it weak and vulnerable. I had seen how hateful things once said and done become part of a storehouse of ugly memories—memories that might grow dim, but never fade completely.

I knew now that we could emerge wiser from our explosions, but not unscathed. There would always be some damage —another rent in the fabric of the relationship. About the best that could be said for the sudden attack upon a child was that it forced one to focus on a situation that needed attention.

I had originally hoped that if I studied the nature of anger, I could permanently immunize myself against my own violent impulses. That may have been a bit of madness, but there was so much that had been remarkable, almost magical, about my work here that I thought, "Why not? Why couldn't I pull off this one last miracle?"

Well I couldn't. And when I came down to earth, I comforted myself. There would be no Nobel Peace Prize for me, but I had won many smaller prizes—all equally precious:

I had learned many specific skills I could depend upon.

I had come to realize that neither I nor my family were as fragile as I had once feared.

I had made peace with the reality that I would never master my anger completely. Each time anger struck, it would come with fresh ferocity. Each time I would find myself struggling to figure out a civilized way to express my savage feelings.

Dr. Ginott was right. It was the work of a lifetime.

Chapter XIII
New Portrait of a Parent

We were glad to see Evelyn back in her accustomed seat again. She had missed the last three sessions. Dr. Ginott greeted her warmly and inquired after her family.

Evelyn smiled wanly. "I suppose the children are all right, but my husband hasn't been well." She then went on to tell us that her husband, Marty, had suffered a heart attack. He was home recuperating now and the doctors were satisfied with his progress, but other problems were presenting themselves.

It seemed that the boys, after the first glow of having their father back from the hospital, had started to complain: 'Daddy isn't the same. He never boxes with us anymore or carries us up to bed. He won't even play baseball with us!'

"You can imagine how that kind of talk depresses Marty," Evelyn said. "I think the pain of his children's disappointment in him is worse than the heart attack. He feels he isn't being a real father to his boys anymore."

Dr. Ginott listened sympathetically. "Evelyn, being a father has nothing to do with boxing or baseball. I know the picture of Dad out there in the park, pitching and catching with his sons, is very attractive. But baseball can be taught by anyone. A father's job is to help his son feel good about himself."

"Feel good about himself?" Evelyn echoed anxiously.

Dr. Ginott elaborated. "A father's most important job is to help his children like themselves—to communicate to them that they're fine human beings, worthy of respect, a pleasure to be with, people whose feelings and ideas have value."

"I wish I had a tape recorder with me," Evelyn sighed. "It would do Marty good to hear that . . . I also wish I knew a way to give some comfort to the boys. This whole experience has been very hard on them. They were terribly upset when their father was taken to the hospital, and now that he's home, there are so many new restrictions upon them. They can't have friends over. They even have to tiptoe around the house and speak in whispers. They're not happy about it, either."

Dr. Ginott spoke with a trace of impatience in his voice. "Evelyn, is it a parent's function to keep his children happy all the time?"

"Not exactly," Evelyn protested, "but no mother wants to see her children looking sad or in tears."

"For me," Dr. Ginott answered, "a child's laughter and his tears have equal importance. I would not want to take away from him disappointment, sorrow, grief. Emotions ennoble character. The deeper we feel, the more human we become."

Evelyn found that hard to accept. "Are you saying that unhappiness can be good for children?"

"I would never plan for unhappiness. But when problems arise I view them as opportunities to teach children that they can become part of the solution. Evelyn, your husband's recuperative period can be a maturing time for your sons. More consideration will be required of them. They'll have to take on extra responsibilities. They can grow from the experience—as long as you don't pollute it for them."

Evelyn looked quizzical. "I'm not sure I understand."

Dr. Ginott said nothing.

Evelyn bit her lip and frowned at the floor. After a few seconds she spoke. "You mean my attitude with the boys can make a difference?"

"What do you think?"

"I think," Evelyn said despondently, "that I've been feeling sorry for them, and that's been making them feel sorry for themselves." Another silence. "I ought to know better by now! You've said a hundred times that our job isn't to make our children happy, but to help them become more human. How often do I have to hear that thought before it becomes part of me?"

Dr. Ginott made a gesture of resignation. "How many times do we have to tune a violin before it stays tuned?"

For a moment Evelyn looked at him uncomprehendingly, then she smiled faintly. Another woman who had been impatiently waiting for an opening, pressed forward with her problem. But I couldn't focus on the discussion that followed. I was stirred by what I had just heard and wanted to think about it some more. . . . Evelyn had come to the meeting with two preconceived notions of what a parent should be—the father who plays ball with his sons, the mother dedicated to her children's happiness. Neither of these notions had been helpful to her or her family. And she would leave today with two very different interpretations of the parents' role, hopefully interpretations that would serve everyone better.

It occurred to me that all of us, in a sense, play a kind of matching game with ourselves. We have a preconceived picture in our heads of what a good parent ought to be and then we try to match ourselves to that picture. When our feelings or behavior coincide with our inner picture, we're content, fulfilled. When they don't, we become anxious, guilty, depressed. Somehow, we feel we've failed our children and ourselves.

I looked around me. One woman was talking animatedly; others were bent forward, listening carefully; a few others were writing in their notebooks. Suddenly I realized that something very important had been going on in this room these past five years. Little by little, we had all been revising our inner picture of the good parent. More than revising! We had been painting an entirely new portrait.

All at once I had a great desire to step back and see the portrait as a whole. Specifically I wanted to know how it differed from the original picture, the one we had started out with. Dr. Ginott had just mentioned some important differences. What were the others?

The first thing that sprang to mind was our attitude toward anger.

We used to think a good parent was a patient parent—calm, logical. He never yelled.

Now we feel no need to bottle up our anger. We express it fully, but instead of hurling insults, we hurl our feelings, our values, our expectations.

We used to think a good parent should always be willing to "do for" his child—help him with his homework, answer all his questions, find solutions to his problems.

Now we know that parents sometimes "help most by not helping—by making themselves dispensable."

We used to think a parent had to be consistent at all costs.

Now we feel freer to have second thoughts, change our minds, live more in terms of our genuine feelings of the moment.

We always thought that some of our negative feelings as parents were "not nice," unreasonable, even shameful.

Now we know that feelings aren't right or wrong. Feelings *are*. What's important is how we deal with what we feel.

So far I liked the picture I saw. Certainly it was less pressured, less guilt-ridden than the old one. A lot kinder to parents. Were the benefits as great for the children?

We never thought it mattered how we spoke to our children, as long as they knew we loved them. What was in our minds was on our tongues.

We still value spontaneity. But now we're aware of the enormous power of our words, and we try to separate what's helpful from what's harmful.

We never knew what to do with our children's strong emotions. We thought we should either tone them down or teach the children to feel differently: "Don't say that, dear. In your heart you really love your sister."

Now we understand that when we acknowledge a child's feelings, we give him health and strength.

We always thought that parents should decide what was best for their children.

Now we know that each time we allow a child to go through the complicated process of making his own decision, we give him an invaluable experience—for now and for his future independence.

It seemed to us that it was the parent's duty to "set the child straight," explain why some of his schemes were foolhardy and unrealistic.

Now we understand that the outside world is only too quick to clip wings, and that it is the parent's privilege to nourish his child's dreams.

We used to think that by telling a child what was wrong with him, he'd improve. If we called him a liar, he'd become honest; if we called him dumb, he'd become smart; if we called him lazy, he'd become industrious.

Now we know that a child's improvement is based upon treating him as if he already *is* what he's capable of becoming.

And that was only a partial list. There were so many other changes in concept that directly affected our behavior. We weren't punishing the children anymore; we weren't sitting in constant judgment upon them; we still insisted, and demanded and expected of them, but always in a way that left their dignity intact.

Dignity! That was the basic difference between the old portrait and the new! The new portrait bestowed infinitely more dignity, upon both parent and child.

My mind traveled back to my own children. Were they aware of all the changes I had been making on their behalf? Could they even begin to appreciate how hard it had been for me to break old patterns and piece together new ones?

I thought of my conversation with Jill yesterday. She had been irritable all evening. At night I sat on her bed and listened to her unburden herself of problem after problem. She had had a fight with her friend, Emily. The class had just started algebra and she didn't understand it. Her social studies report on the rise of Nazi Germany was due in two days and she hadn't even started it yet.

My old inner "good parent" picture was immediately activated. "What kind of mother are you?" it urged. "Don't just sit there. Your child is unhappy. Do something! Reassure her about the algebra. Tell her she's bright and that she'll get it in time. Warn her not to leave her reports for the last minute again. As far as Emily is concerned, advise her to let bygones be bygones."

But I also had access to another picture, a newer one, and luckily it prevailed over the old. So I just sat there, saying little, hearing all her thoughts and feelings—some of them over and over again. Slowly she began to explore a few possible solutions. Again, I just listened. Then tentatively, I offered a suggestion of my own. Nothing was resolved, but after a while I could see the tautness go out of her body. As I tucked her in, I said, "Well, you've certainly had a lot to wrestle with."

She seized my hand for a moment and held it. I kissed her, closed the light, and started to leave.

Jill called me back. "Mom?"

"Yes?"

In the darkened room I could almost feel her searching for a way to tell me what was in her heart. When she finally spoke, her voice was solemn. "I can talk to you. . . . Do you know what I think?"

"What?"

"I think if Hitler had you for a mother, he wouldn't have been Hitler."

I smiled. Did she really believe that her mother could singlehandedly reverse the course of history?

Then I reconsidered her "compliment." Actually Jill was paying tribute, not just to her particular mother, but to a way of relating between human beings, a way that had deeply affected her, and her family.

Slowly it dawned upon me. My guileless child might be right. And if she were, if the loving feelings generated by this process really were enough to prevent a Hitler—why there'd be hope for almost anyone!

I bent over and kissed her once more. "Young lady," I said, "you've given me much to think about. Goodnight."

Index